# SPANISH CIVIL WAR
# BLOCKADE RUNNERS

**by**
**Paul Heaton**

P.M. Heaton Publishing
Abergavenny, Monmouthshire
Great Britain
2006

*Front Cover:* The tanker *English Tanker* which was bombed and sunk at Alicante on June 6, 1938. Although flying the British flag and registered at Newcastle, she was actually owned by Republicans at Madrid. After the Civil War ended, on April 26, 1939 she was raised, repaired and entered the Spanish fleet as the *Castillo Almenara.*

*(Laurence Dunn Collection).*

*Back Cover:* The British steamer *Farnham* was bombed and sunk at Alicante on June 27, 1938. She was owned by the Alpha Steamship Co. Ltd., of London. On August 27, 1939 she was refloated and following repairs became the Spanish *Castillo Montiel.*

*(Laurence Dunn Collection).*

*Frontispiece:* The steamer *Seven Seas Spray* which broke the Blockade of Bilbao on April 20, 1937. The Cardiff registered vessel is shown here under her later name of *Seabank Spray* but still owned by Alfred Pope of Porthcawl.

*(Welsh Industrial & Maritime Museum).*

*Page 6:* Map of Spain showing the territory taken by the Nationalists at various stages of the Civil War.

*Pages 4 & 5:* Original watercolour by Commander D.H. Edleston, depicting the capture of Lord Glanely's steamer *Molton* off Santander on July 14, 1937 by the Nationalist cruiser *Almirante Cervera* within sight of HMS *Royal Oak.* The artist was serving on board the *Royal Oak* and witnessed the incident.

ISBN: 1 872006 21 3
© First Edition June, 2006

Published by P.M. Heaton Publishing
Abergavenny, Monmouthshire, NP7 8NG


Printed in Great Britain by
The Amadeus Press
Cleckheaton, West Yorkshire, BD19 4TQ


Typesetting and page layout by
Highlight Type Bureau Ltd, Bradford, BD8 7BY

Vivan los Marineros Ingles
Viva la Libertad


Long live English Sailors
Long live Liberty


The People of Bilbao,
April 20, 1937

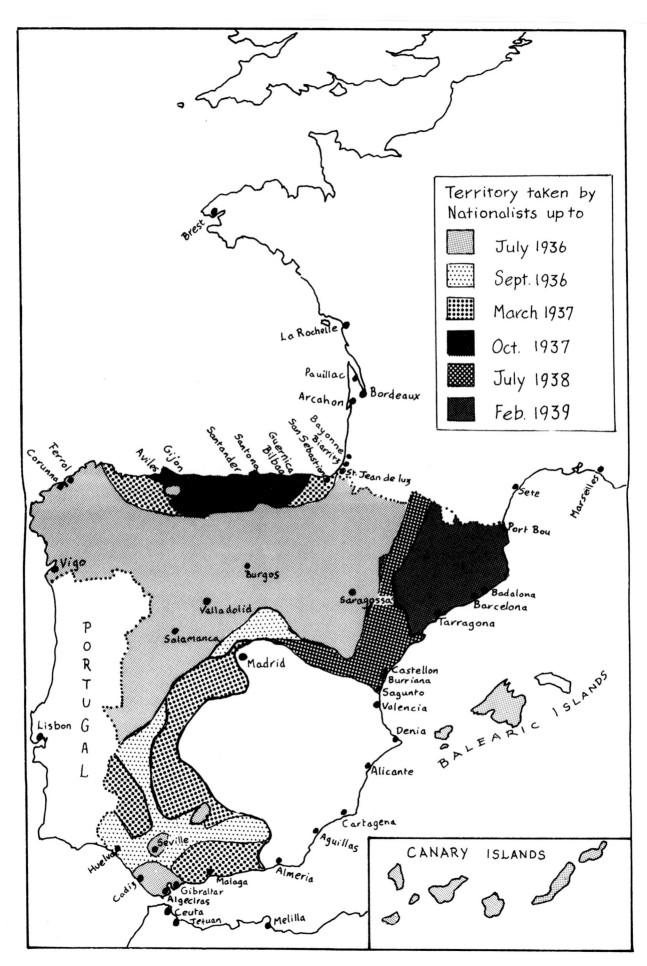

Territory taken by
Nationalists up to

July 1936

Sept. 1936

March 1937

Oct. 1937

July 1938

Feb. 1939

Brest

La Rochelle

Pauillac

Arcahon

Bordeaux

Bayonne

Biarritz

San Sebastian

St. Jean de luz

Sete

Marseilles

Port Bou

Ferrol

Corunna

Aviles

Gijon

Santander

Santona

Guernica

Bilbao

Vigo

Burgos

Saragossa

Badalona

Barcelona

Valladolid

Tarragona

Salamanca

P O R T U G A L

Madrid

Castellon

Burriana

Sagunto

Valencia

Denia

B A L E A R I C   I S L A N D S

Lisbon

Alicante

Cartagena

Aguillas

Seville

Almeria

Huelva

Malaga

Cadiz

Gibraltar

Algeciras

Ceuta

Tetuan

Melilla

CANARY   ISLANDS

# ACKNOWLEDGEMENTS

I would like to thank all those who have helped in the compilation of this volume, particularly:–

Messrs. H.S. Appleyard, D. Burrell, C.J.M. Carter, J. Clarkson, J. Cook, A. Duncan, L. Dunn, F.W. Hawks, K.H. King, F.W. Jones, H.S. Jones, K. O'Donoghue, E.N. Taylor, R. Wiltshire, J.J. Wright, D. Robinson, Cdr. D.H. Eddleston, Mrs. O.A. Roberts, Miss M. Urresti, the National Museum of Wales – Welsh Industrial & Maritime Museum, Cardiff Central, Newport and Cwmbran Reference Libraries, World Ship Society Central Record Team, World Ship Photo Library, and Hugh Thomas regarding his book *The Spanish Civil War*.

# BIBLIOGRAPHY

Appleyard, H.S. and Heaton, P.M. – The Baron Glanely of St. Fagans and W.J. Tatam Ltd. (World Ship Society, 1980).

Daily Mail for the period.

Edleston Cdr. D.H. – Personal recollections.

Echegaray, R.G. – La Marina Mercante y el Trafico Maritimo en la Guerra Civil (Libreria Editorial San Martin).

Francis, H. – Miners Against Fascism (Lawrence and Wishart, 1984).

Gibbs, J.M. – Morels of Cardiff (National Museum of Wales, 1982).

Heaton, P.M. – The Usk Ships (Author, 1982).

Heaton, P.M. – The Abbey Line (Author, 1983).

Heaton, P.M. – The South American Saint Line (Author, 1985).

Heaton, P.M. – Welsh Blockade Runners in the Spanish Civil War (Author, 1985).

Heaton, P.M. – Tatems of Cardiff (Author, 1987).

Heaton, P.M. – Jack Billmeir, Merchant Shipowner (Author, 1989).

Jackson, G. – A Concise History of the Spanish Civil War (Thomas and Hudson, 1974).

Jones, F.W. – Personal Recollections.

Jones, H.S. – Personal Recollections.

Lloyd's List for the period.

Lloyd's Register of Shipping for the period.

Lloyd's Weekly Casualty Reports for the period.

McAlister, A.S. and Gray, L. – H. Hogarth and Sons Ltd – Baron Line (World Ship Society, 1976).

Patton, W. – The Scrap Log of an Engineer (A.H. Stockwell).

Thomas, H. – The Spanish Civil War (Eyre and Spottiswoode, 1961).

Times for the period.

Vella, Philip – Malta: Blitzed But Not Beaten (Progress Press, Valletta, for the National War Museum Association, 1985).

Western Mail for the period.

# CONTENTS

# INTRODUCTION

Mention the Spanish Civil War to anyone and they will generally think of that conflict in Spain before the Second World War in which the International Brigades fought. At one time I knew little more about the subject myself. However, having been engaged in compiling histories of a number of South Wales shipowners I noted almost with frustration that the topic kept cropping up in my conversations with those connected with the industry. The name 'Potato' Jones was quoted time and again, and eventually I decided that it was time to find out what the Spanish Civil War was all about, and who this character 'Potato' Jones was. As a result my researches appeared in the book *Welsh Blockade Runners in the Spanish Civil War* (1985). This work has long since been out of print and I am often asked if I would consider reprinting the book. Whilst I have continued to study the subject I believe it to be more appropriate to produce an expanded volume dealing with all the vessels involved, including other British ships, but drawing heavily on the original material together with some of my subsequent work.

On July 18, 1936 a rebellion occurred in Spain when the majority of the Armed Forces aided by the Right wing of Spanish politics set about overthrowing the lawfully elected Popular Front or Republican Government which was supported by the Left. Within a month of the outbreak of hostilities half of Spain was in the hands of troops under the control of General Franco. The insurgents or rebels later became known as the Nationalists and were often referred to as the Salamanca or Burgos Government. The Republic Government was often referred to by the right wing British Press as the 'Reds', but generally were better known as the Republicans, the Madrid Government, and after the move from that besieged city, as the Valencia Government.

Trade between the United Kingdom and Spain was important to both countries. They needed our coal and we needed their iron ore and pyrites. The iron ore mines around Bilbao were the source of much of the United Kingdom's supplies, and indeed the mines had in decades past been owned by such South Wales firms as the Ebbw Vale Iron Company, the Dowlais Iron Company, Morel and Company and John Cory and Sons. The mineral deposits at Huelva were still owned in 1936 by the British 'Rio Tinto' company.

Much of the coal exported to Spain came from the South Wales valleys and was shipped from ports such as Newport, Cardiff, Penarth, Barry, Port Talbot and Swansea, and a large proportion of the cargo in each direction was carried in ships owned and / or managed in Wales.

As a result of the war the trade which had hitherto been carried on with a united Spain was now being undertaken with two distinct zones. The insurgents quickly gained control of the sea around Spain and started to exercise a form of influence on foreign (including British) shipping. Apart from an attempted blockade of the insurgent held Cadiz by the Republicans early in the war they had little effect on shipping going to and from ports under the control of General Franco's forces. However, the insurgents from an early stage in the conflict were able to interfere with some of the shipments on route to the Republic.

Ships flying the Spanish Republican flag were being captured and sunk by the insurgent forces. One vessel was even shelled and sunk in the North Sea off Great Yarmouth. The insurgent's interference with these vessels and those flying other flags resulted in an increase in shipments on ships flying the British flag. Non intervention was proposed and after a fashion implemented by the Great Powers, but support for the insurgents was still provided by Germany, Italy and to a lesser extent by Portugal. The Republic was actively supported by Russia and again to a lesser extent by France.

The increase in shipments to the Republicans in British ships resulted in a problem for the British Government, in that whilst privately preferring a Franco style government, they had proposed non intervention. British ships were carrying the vast majority of the cargo and the insurgents controlled the waters around Spain. This meant that it was the insurgents who were stopping the ships, and British ships that they were stopping. The result was to see a higher level of protection being provided outside Spanish Territorial Waters by the Royal Navy than had previously been needed.

Many incidents were reported of British and neutral ships being attacked, damaged, captured and sunk, and it is in relation to the activities of these merchant ships that this book is concerned. I have started with a review of what the war was about and thereafter outlined the involvement of merchant ships throughout each stage of the conflict.

I hope that you enjoy this book as much as I have enjoyed writing it.

Paul Heaton
June, 2006

though this was flagrantly ignored by Italy, Germany and Russia. The naval patrols set up to enforce the embargo affected mainly the government side. What seaborne supplies that came to them were subject to attack from the air and "unknown submarines" (known then and proved later to be Italian). Since the insurgents controlled the wheatlands, the Republicans were short of food and in the last year of the Civil War the rations were at near starvation level.

The British mercantile marine (and that of other European countries) still affected by the effects of the depression of the early 1930s were eager to capture what trade was available, despite the British Baldwin Government's attempts to deter this. It was this situation which underlies the events recounted in this book.


* Welsh Blockade Runners in the Spanish Civil War – P.M. Heaton (1985)

## Chapter 2
# OUTBREAK OF WAR

With the commencement of the rebellion on July 18, 1936 the insurgents quickly seized control of the Northern part of the country to the North of Madrid, with the exception of the area near to the coast stretching from Gijon in the West to Bilbao in the East. The Balearics (with the exception of Minorca), the Canary Islands, and Spanish Morocco quickly fell to the rebels, but the rebellion at Madrid itself and at Barcelona was successfully put down by troops remaining loyal to the Government. A state of utter confusion reigned throughout the country, and in some areas strikes were called by the government itself in an effort to halt the progress of the insurgents. On the coast, the area on the Atlantic coast to the West of Gibraltar fell to the insurgents within a day or two, giving them the ports of Huelva, Cadiz and Algeciras. Attempts were made to transport troops from Morocco to these ports by sea, but initially the Government were able to command control of the Straits of Gibraltar and many of those attempting to cross were lost or captured. For this reason General Franco, who had flown to Spanish Morocco at the outbreak of the rebellion, made approaches to Hitler and Mussolini, for help, and transport aircraft were quickly placed at his disposal. It was in this way that the Army of Africa arrived in mainland Spain, and in time to ensure the momentum of the conflict was maintained by the insurgents.

In the North the ports of Vigo and Corunna fell to the insurgents in the early days of the conflict followed by Ferrol and Rivadeo. Two British ships held up at Corunna by strikes at the time of the outbreak of hostilities were the *Ottinge* owned by Constants (South Wales) Ltd., and the Newcastle registered steamer *Hillfern* which was controlled by Claude Angel of Cardiff. Both ships were subjected to air attack, and whilst the former was undamaged the *Hillfern* was hit by machine gun fire whilst docked at the inner harbour on July 20. She received damage to her bridge, port holes and her whistle steam pipe, but no casualties were reported amongst her crew.

At the outbreak of the Spanish Civil War, the steamer *Ottinge* was strike bound at Corunna. The vessel survived an air attack on the port on July 20, 1936 and was undamaged.                    *(Welsh Industrial & Maritime Museum)*

Two further views of the Abbey Line's steamer *Melrose Abbey* at anchor at Las Palmas in July, 1936.

Early on the morning of July 25 Ceuta was bombarded by Spanish Government (Republican) warships, including the *Jaime I*, and the cruisers *Libertad* and *Miguel De Cervantes*. Whilst considerable damage was caused on shore, the rebel guns firing from Ceuta were successful in hitting and damaging the bows of the *Jaime I*.

On the 27th the French steamer *Saumur* was bombed but undamaged in the Straits of Gibraltar. She had been on passage from Algiers for Bordeaux and La Rochelle with a general cargo. Four bombs had fallen near her, two within 50 yards.

The following day, as the Bland steamer *Gibel Zerjon* was about to enter Gibraltar from Tangier she was narrowly missed by shells which were aimed at two Republican submarines on the surface near her when the insurgent fortress at Algeciras across the bay opened fire.

During this period a considerable number of foreign nationals were evacuated from war-torn areas of Spain. Royal Navy vessels naturally carrying British subjects to Gibraltar and French ports, and other naval vessels embarking a wide range of nationalities in similar fashion.

On August 5 the destroyer HMS *Basilisk* arrived at Gibraltar from Almeria and reported that she had been fired on enroute. It was thought that the forts at Ceuta had, in the mist, mistaken her for a Republican vessel, and fortunately their shells had missed.

On August 7 the insurgent cruiser *Almirante Cervera* had shelled Gijon in the North hoping to gain access to the sea at this point for their troops. Two days of heavy bombardment was to flatten the town with the loss of many hundreds of innocent civilian lives. On the same day the Republican battleship *Jaime Primero* and a cruiser of the *Libertad* class had bombarded Ceuta, and then moved on to attack Algeciras, destroying the insurgent warship *Dato* in the harbour. The Dutch liner *Dempo* which was in the area was lucky not to be hit by the return fire from the shore batteries.

On the same day the Italian steamer *Dante* had a lucky escape when bombed a few miles East of Gibraltar by insurgent aircraft, but was not hit.

A tragedy took place in the North when the master of the British yacht *Blue Shadow*, Captain Rupert Savile was killed and his wife injured by a shell fired by the insurgent cruiser *Almirante Cervera* off Gijon, on August 9. The yacht had been proceeding to Oporto from Bilbao when one of its screws went wrong, and it was necessary to put into port. Through the intermediary of the British Authorities Captain Savile had obtained leave to take his vessel into Gijon, but on arriving there she was caught in the fire from the Republican batteries on shore. He then instructed his men to make for the protection of the British destroyer HMS *Comet*, which was lying off the coast, and a shell fell on the poop, killing Captain Savile. The crew succeeded in bringing the yacht alongside HMS *Comet*. The *Comet* then conveyed Mrs Savile who had been injured by shrapnel and the body of her late husband to the French Bay of Biscay port of St. Jean de Luz, while the damaged yacht was left at anchor in the port of Musel.

It was reported on August 10 at Gibraltar that the ferry *Margarita II* had been hit twice by shells the previous day, but the extent of damage is unknown to me.

In mid-August the insurgent naval forces intensified their bombardment of Republican (Basque) territory. The cruisers, *Almirante Cervera*, *Velasco* and the battleship *Espana* being particularly active. Much damage was inflicted on San Sebastian, Guadalupa and Fuenterrabia.

A Republican success was heralded in the North on August 18 when a 500 ton steamer, *El Tiburon*, fitted out and armed as a privateer was captured by forces off Santander. She had been used to obtain supplies for the *Almirante Cervera*, and was armed with guns fore and aft to protect her from submarine attacks. A naval officer Lt. Montajo was in command. She was located by a Republican aircraft who communicated with the shore, and trawlers and fishing smacks were sent at once in pursuit. The *El Tiburon* was eventually put out of action by bombs from the plane. With her engine-room wrecked and her guns silenced she was boarded by the fishermen, who however, lost a number of men from rifle fire. Two lifeboats from the *Almirante Cervera* were found on board the vessel, which was towed into Santander.

In the South on August 19 a Republican cruiser stopped the German steamer *Kamerun* seven miles off Cadiz by firing three shells across her bows. The *Kamerun* was due to call at Cadiz to evacuate German refugees and take them to Genoa. She was searched and then allowed to proceed, but was ordered not to enter the port of Cadiz. On the same day the *Libertad* tried to prevent the Swedish steamer *Gallia* from entering Cadiz to load. However the military authorities at Cadiz intervened and the vessel entered port.

Three days later the Bland steamer *Gibel Zerjon*, which carried freight and passengers between Gibraltar and Morocco, had been stopped by the Republican cruiser *Miguel de Cervantes*. The Royal Navy had sent the vessels *Cordington* and *Repulse* from Gibraltar to investigate. Eventually the Bland ship made Melilia, her intended

Meanwhile the crews of British ships engaged in the Spanish trade made a demand for a 50% bonus on wages while 'in danger' at Spanish ports and on January 5 held up the departure of the British steamers *Lilburn* and *Macgregor* at Cardiff. A similar claim was made by the crews of other British ships trading in Spanish waters. The men demanded that 'danger money' should be payable 24 hours before a vessel arrives at a Spanish port until 24 hours after leaving. The district secretary of the National Seamen's Union said that the crews on the *Lilburn* and *Macgregor* refused to sign on until they had an assurance concerning the bonus, but the crew of another vessel the *Heminge* had signed on pending a settlement.

The dispute was soon settled, and the fairness of the men's demand can be gauged in that it was met in full.

The *Macgregor* dating from 1919 with a gross tonnage of 2,498 was one of three vessels acquired in 1936 by the Guardian Line Ltd., of Atlantic Buildings, Mount Stuart Square, Cardiff. The company which was formed in 1932, was managed by Charles Alan Roberts, who in 1940 became responsible for managing the vessels of Morel Ltd., of Cardiff. The *Macgregor* which was registered at Ardrossan, was to be heavily involved in the Spanish trade, whilst the *Heminge* owned by Constants, was to serve ports under the control of the Nationalist (insurgent) side.

Further Russian cargo ships were being stopped and inspected by insurgent forces. The steamer *Krasny Profintern* was stopped near Gibraltar and taken into Ceuta. The vessel carrying a cargo of coal from Bremen to Naples, was released later the same day, and proceeded on her voyage. Not so lucky was the Russian steamer *Smidovitch* which was captured in the Bay of Biscay by the insurgent destroyer *Velasco*. This ship which had left Leningrad with a cargo of foodstuffs sold by the All-Union Exports Association to Spanish Republican trade organisations, had a cargo comprising 1,850 tons of rye, 919 tons of lentils and 572 tons of wheat. The Russian ship was taken into Pasajes where her cargo was seized and crew imprisoned. Eventually the crew were repatriated, but the ship was kept by the Nationalists who named her *Castillo Penafiel* and registered her appropriately at Pasajes.

Two other Russian ships stopped in the South, were the *Rosa Luxemburg* which was taken into Ceuta, and the *Sakhalin* which was taken to Ferrol. Both were carrying coal from Rotterdam for Italy, and were soon released. Shortly after the *Vtoraya Pyatiletka* bound West was stopped and taken into Ceuta for inspection. The master of the Russian *Maxim Gorky* which was taken into Ceuta on January 10 was told before his ship was released, that the crew of the *Komsomol* which had been shelled and sunk a month earlier were still alive and imprisoned in Spanish Morocco, and subsequently reported this to Moscow.

At this time a Spanish steamer, the *Jose Tartiere* which had left Valencia on December 26 for Bilbao, was chased along the Basque coast, and having made good her escape put into the safety of the French port of St. Nazaire.

The Norwegian steamer *Iris* was stopped, but on this occasion, this ship was taken to Algeciras, where following the inspection of her cargo and papers she was released a day later. The French *Ville de Bastia* was stopped by insurgent trawlers off Cape Finisterre and again the following day off Cape Silliero. But on both occasions having proved the vessels nationality was allowed to proceed.

The Spanish motor vessel *Villa de Madrid* bound from Marseilles for Alicante took refuge at Valencia following an attack by a submarine near Cullera. The same day another Spanish vessel, the *Ciudad de Barcelona* was attacked by a submarine near Cape San Antonio but made it to the safety of Alicante.

On January 11 Malaga was the target of a heavy bombardment from land and sea. Considerable damage was done and many casualties, estimated at 300 were caused. The Danish steamer *Signe* and the Norwegian steamer *Saga* were alongside the quay at Malaga Harbour waiting to load fruit, when six insurgent aircraft dropped 100 incendiary bombs all over the town, at the same time two cruisers fired over 200 shells at Malaga. Both merchant ships, which had steam up, lost no time in leaving for the safety of Gibraltar. Splinters of shells had hit both vessels, and some of the crews had received slight injuries which received treatment ashore at Gibraltar.

Claude Angel's Newport registered steamer *Bramhill* (1,834 gross tons) had left Barcelona on January 6 and after touching Tarragona to complete her cargo she called at Gibraltar for bunkers and on January 12 was off Cape Tarife just West of the Straits of Gibraltar when she was approached by the armed insurgent trawler *Larache* which fired a shot at her. The *Bramhill* slowed up and immediately sent out a wireless message for assistance. This call was answered by the British cruiser HMS *Sussex* which went to her aid. The *Sussex* requested the rebel trawler to leave, which she did. Thereafter the captain of the *Sussex* caused the papers of the *Bramhill* to be inspected. The ship was carrying a general cargo, and following the inspection she was allowed to proceed on her voyage to Bilbao.

The feelings of the French towards Franco and his German and Italian friends was clearly shown in January when the dockers refused to unload the German steamer *Indra* for eight days. Her cargo of pyrites had been brought from Huelva to Marseilles, and it was only unloaded after it had been pointed out that the supply of pyrites was needed by

France for reasons of national defence.

In the North the insurgent warships *Espana* and *Velasco* stopped the Norwegian steamer *Hild* off Santander. The Norwegian crew were questioned for around half an hour, and the vessel was allowed to proceed after making sure that she carried no cargo for Santander.

Since the start of the civil war, a number of trawlers, mostly registered at Vigo, had been moored in the Bay of Gibraltar. They were handed over to insurgent authorities after debt incurred on the trawlers had been paid. These vessels which were then quickly removed to insurgent territory, were the *Masso Nueve, Masso Diez, Masso Once, Mondego, Tiburon, Meira, San Fausto,* and *San Gregorio.*

On January 16 the Danish steamer *Nordsoen* was stopped in the Straits and taken into Ceuta by insurgent gunboats. She was carrying a cargo of arms for Valencia, and had her cargo confiscated, before she was allowed to leave, making for Oran to bunker. Thereafter she continued her voyage to Valencia to report the loss of her cargo.

On the same day three Russian ships were stopped in the Straits and taken to Ceuta for examination. These were the motor vessel *Volga*, which was released a day later, and the steamers *Kara* and *Revolyutsioner* which were freed after a few hours detention.

The following Russian ships were all detained at Ceuta in the next day or so, but having nothing to do with trade to Spain were all released. They were the *Pokrovsky* bound for Calais, *Lunacharski* for Boulogne, *Vtoraya Pyattletka* for Boston, *Transbalt* for Antwerp, *Petrovsky* for Birkenhead, *Budeny* bound from Rotterdam for Italy, and the *Neva* for London, Rotterdam and Hamburg. On January 19 the Russian steamer *Dekabrist*, Poti for Gdynia with a cargo of ore was stopped within seven miles of Gibraltar and taken into Ceuta for inspection.

On January 19 an insurgent submarine attempted to torpedo the Spanish merchantman *J.J. Sister* off Tarragona. None of the torpedoes struck the vessel which escaped. The torpedoes fired at her hit a reef near a light-house.

The next day the Swedish steamer *Isa* was stopped and released when it was proved that she was bound for Hamburg. Two further Russian ships were taken to Ceuta for examination, the *Ural Masch* bound from Antwerp to Savona, and the *Dickson* bound West. Both were subsequently released.

Meanwhile, the Association representing Scandinavian seamen instructed their members not to proceed on voyages to Spain due to the danger. As a result even vessels actually enroute when making port had the problem of crews who would go no further. On January 20 the crew of the Norwegian *Sneland I* which was loading coal at Cardiff for Seville refused to sail on the vessel. At Leith the Norwegian *Gaston Micard* which was due to sail for Spain, did not sail when the owners cancelled the contract. The *Maria Toft* flying the Danish flag was due to carry a cargo of coal from Cardiff to Vigo became strike bound. The crew of the Finnish steamer *Savonia* demanded to be paid-off at Cardiff as the vessel was about to sail for Vigo.

The Spanish motor vessel *Araya Mendi* which was proceeding towards Malaga noted two insurgent warships going towards Malaga. These ships bombarded the town and then without warning turned their fire on the merchant ship, which had got as far to the coast as possible. The ship then ran aground, but was subjected to shelling for about 30 minutes. Her passengers were safely landed, but she had some damage to her hull and engines. Minor repairs were effected, and the ship was able to refloat without the aid of tugs and arrived at Malaga. Unfortunately during a subsequent air raid the ship was struck by a bomb, but the damage was not serious.

The Spanish steamer *Cabo Sacratif*, which was carrying women and children from the Malaga front, had to run for safety when the periscope of a submarine was seen by the crew. The steamer was then about three miles from Tarragona and according to the crew the submarine was only 50 yards away when the master gave orders for her to change her course for Tarragona. The submarine followed for a distance, but with the steamer sounding his siren the Republican aircraft sent to investigate could find no trace of the offending craft.

The Russian steamer *Tiflis* was stopped in the Straits on January 21 and taken to Ceuta for examination, but later allowed to proceed. At this time a Greek steamer had her cargo confiscated at the same port before being freed.

The following day the Norwegian steamer *Carrier* which was waiting outside Aviles with a cargo of blende for a mining company was ordered to follow the insurgent warship *Estaca de Bares*. The vessel was taken at first to Ferrol where part of her cargo was unloaded and thence to Corunna where the remainder was seized.

The Greek steamer *Rita* which had taken the cargo from the Spanish vessel *Cabo Silleiro* at Casablanca was enroute to Barcelona when she was captured and taken to Ceuta where part of her coal cargo was discharged. The vessel was then sailed under guard for Cadiz where the remainder of the coal was unloaded for the Nationalist cause.

On January 27 the Spanish steamer *Tramontana* arrived at Marseilles where her cargo consisting of 22,680 kilograms of gold and one case of jewels worth six million francs was unloaded. Clearly the Republic did not want

On March 5 the Spanish steamer *Legazpi* which had left Rosas for Barcelona was attacked by insurgent aircraft. The attack was so fierce that the crew jumped overboard into the sea, and the vessel undamaged went aground near Cape San Sebastian on Llefrach Beach. Subsequently the crew reboarded and succeeded in refloating the ship.

Further neutral ships were stopped in the Straits and escorted under arms to Ceuta for examination, these included the Belgian *Henri Gerlinger* whose detention lasted for only a few hours. The Danish steamers *Edith* and *Kirsten* were freed following a detailed examination. However the Norwegian *Breidablik* and *Erica* had their cargoes of fruit confiscated before being allowed to leave. Both these ships masters made for Gibraltar where they complained that they were only allowed to leave with 15 tons of bunkers, just sufficient to make Gibraltar to rebunker.

The British steamer *Springwear* bound for Alicante was hailed by an insurgent armed trawler and ordered to proceed to Ceuta. The master refused to submit and made for the safety of Gibraltar at full speed.

On March 8 a series of SOS messages were received by Land's End Wireless Station from an unknown vessel – 'SOS lat.45.10N, long. 3.20W, fire on board, sinking'. A later repeat of this message gave the identity of the vessel in distress as the *'Adda'* of Newcastle. As a result of this message the Royal Navy dispatched four warships to the area to assist. HMS *Echo*, HMS *Eclipse*, HMS *Encounter* and HMS *Escapade*. It transpired that the identity given for this merchant ship was bogus, and that she was in fact the Spanish Republican motor vessel *Mar Cantabrico* which had been intercepted by the insurgent cruiser *Canarias* which had shelled and set the ship on fire 50 miles North West of Bordeaux. The ship was boarded by a party from the *Canarias* who imprisoned many of the crew together with Mexican and Italian passengers transferring them to the warship.

The *Mar Cantabrico* had left New York in January with a cargo of eight aircraft and took on munitions at Vera Cruz, Mexico leaving for Spain in February, and had been intercepted by the insurgent cruiser in the Bay of Biscay, who would have been well aware of the passage of this vessel.

The report issued by the British United Press helps to sort out some of the confusion regarding this incident:–

> Pablo Juan Boo, a Spanish seaman, and an uncaptured survivor of the motor vessel *Mar Cantabrico* was landed in Arcachon today (March 9, 1937) by the French trawler *Henri Cameleyre*. He asserted that the *Mar Cantabrico* did not sink, that the fire was partly extinguished, and that the vessel was towed away towards San Sebastian. "There were 150 people on board", he said, "11 of these were drowned while trying to escape". He said, "We were 50 miles from Arcachon when we sighted the warship *Canarias*. We changed our direction and headed for Bilbao, but the *Canarias* was faster and chased us and torpedoed us. We were unarmed and could not return the fire. A shell from the *Canarias* set fire to our ship amidships. The *Canarias* sent out boats and put sailors on board the *Mar Cantabrico*, and she took charge of her and partly extinguished the fire. Escorted by the *Canarias* and manned by sailors from the cruiser the *Mar Cantabrico* headed for San Sebastian, partly under her own power. She was carrying five 'planes but a considerable quantity of munitions.

Pablo Juan Boo gave himself up to the French authorities. The insurgents stated that the members of the crew of the vessel who had been captured by the *Canarias* included ten North Americans, some of whom were Mexicans, and fifteen Italians. The remainder of the crew were Spaniards; there were no passengers.

The Spanish seaman – Pablo Juan Boo further stated to Reuter:–

> A shell from the cruiser *Canarias* struck No. 2 hold of the *Mar Cantabrico* and started a fire. It was then that we sent out the SOS using the signal of the vessel whose name we had borrowed. A number of boats were put out from the *Canarias* and the insurgent officers carried out a search. Finally the crew were taken on board the cruiser. We left New York in January with eight 'planes at the moment when congress was discussing the arms embargo. We stopped at Vera Cruz to take on further arms and did not arrive in the Bay of Biscay until Monday (March 8).

The damaged merchant ship was taken into the insurgent port of Pasajes. A few days later French fishing vessels reported picking up two bodies of members of the crew. Both had been shot in the head.

On March 9 the Catalan authorities ordered the sinking of the *Marie Therese le Borgne*, a French vessel which had struck a floating mine a week earlier and been beached near the little port of Palamos, about 60 miles North-east of Barcelona. When the master and his 22 crew were repatriated to France, he complained that as they had tried to refloat the ship an aircraft had attacked them, slightly injuring the First Mate.

Further neutral ships were stopped in the Straits of Gibraltar, including the Norwegian *Rolf Jarl* and the Danish *Ebba*, which after inspection at Ceuta, were soon released.

On March 10 an insurgent armed trawler had attacked the Spanish Republican steamer *Conde de Zubiria* off Ushant.

The Ushant semaphore lookout saw the attack and informed the Maritime Prefect at Brest who ordered a seaplane to the spot. The 'plane flew over the trawler, which thereupon fled before a coastguard cutter could reach the spot. The steamer first took refuge in a small bay, and then put into Brest. She was not damaged.

The stopping of the Dutch steamer *Triton* by an insurgent armed trawler in the Straits of Gibraltar caused an outrage in the Netherland Parliament. The ship which was enroute from Barcelona to Holland with a cargo of fruit was directed into Ceuta under force of arms, where her cargo of 200 tons of piece goods and 30,000 cases of oranges was confiscated and the crew had the unenviable tasks of unloading it, before the ship was allowed to proceed. The Dutch cruiser *Java* was ordered to proceed to Spanish waters in order to protect Dutch shipping on the high seas.

The French steamer *Djebel Antar* was bombed from the air when about 115 miles East of Majorca. Some material damage was done, but no one was injured. There were no passengers on the vessel which was on the service from Philippeville to Marseilles. The ship proceeded on her course.

The Estonian steamer *Olev* bound for Bayonne (France) from Barry was stopped by insurgent warships off the French coast and escorted to Pasajes, where following examination was released. The Finnish steamer *Hildegaard* bound from Gdynia for Batum was stopped and taken into Ceuta, but was freed the following day.

The steamer *Minerva* of Mariehamn, Follonica for Rotterdam with a cargo of ore was stopped by insurgents and taken to Ceuta where the cargo was examined, before her release.

Meanwhile the steamer *Springwear* which had entered Gibraltar having failed to submit to an insurgent gunboat a week or more ago was brought inside the Admiralty Harbour, where she was ordered to discharge her cargo of 1,400 tons of wheat into lighters in the presence of port and revenue officials. This search was made at the insistence of the Naval Authorities at Gibraltar in answer to a Nationalist allegation that she was carrying war materials. Nothing was found and her cargo was reloaded, and the ship left on March 19, following a formal protest being made by the master at the unnecessary delay.

The Dutch steamer *Serooskerk* was seized in the Straits by insurgent naval forces and taken to Ceuta. She had been on a voyage from Rotterdam for the Far East, but was later released. The Dutch Charge d'Affaires at Tangier lodged an emphatic protest in the name of the Dutch Government against the seizure of Dutch vessels. The Dutch cruiser had yet to arrive in the region.

The Norwegian steamer *Makefjell* arrived at Gibraltar from Ceuta on March 13 having lost her cargo to the insurgents. At the same time the Swedish *Mauritz* docked also from Ceuta. The Danish steamer *Dorrit* was taken into Ceuta but released following inspection of her cargo. Three other vessels which were subsequently released following the confiscation of their cargoes were the Belgian *Henri Gerlinger* and *Prina* and the Danish *Polly*.

The Dutch steamer *Jonge Johanna* bound for Sete with a cargo of coal was seized by insurgents and taken into Ceuta. The Dutch warship *Hertog Hendrik* arrived on the scene too late to prevent the vessel being taken. The merchant ship did not avail itself of the convoy facilities offered by Dutch warships which became effective on that day (March 17). In the event the vessel was later released with her cargo intact.

The French steamer *Djebel Antar* was attacked for a second time in the Mediterranean and the master gave the following details of the damage, 'one bomb fell on the deck, pierced the iron plating and two partitions, finishing up in an empty hold. As a result of this incident four French cruisers were sent out of Toulon on patrol duty – two patrolling between Sardina and the Balearic Islands, and two off the Algerian coast. Clearly another nation was being irritated by Nationalist (insurgent) activity.

The Norwegian steamer *Trajan* arrived at Oran following a short detention at Ceuta.

At midnight on March 13 the Non-Intervention Committee's scheme for the supervision of the land and sea boundaries of Spain came into force. The steps announced in connection with the sea control plan included:–

Brest:– The French destroyer *Fantasque* sailed for the Spanish coast. The destroyer *Jaguar*, flagship of Admiral Brohan, and five torpedo-boats are also preparing to leave.

Perpignan:– The French cruiser *Intrepide* will in future be stationed at Port Vendres, on the Mediterranean coast. She will, at the same time, act as a convoy to liners bound from Port Vendres to Algiers and Oran. The cruiser will escort them halfway both on their outward and inward voyages. The squadron stationed off Algeria will then take over. It was announced in Berlin that a flotilla of armed fishing trawlers had been formed and will be attached to the German fleet as from March 14 to help in the supervision scheme. Latest plans for controlling the Franco-Spanish and the Spanish-Portuguese frontiers include: Dividing the Franco-Spanish frontier into three zones, each under an administrator, who will be assisted by 130 observers, with headquarters in Paris; and setting up of two main zones to control the Spanish-Portuguese frontier. Lisbon to control the South and Oporto the North.

The Norwegian steamer *Vigor*, Jaffa for Southampton, cargo oranges, was seized by insurgents in the Straits of Gibraltar and taken to Ceuta for examination. The British Foreign Office sent a strong protest to General Franco. It emphasised that the *Vigor*, like many other of the seized vessels, especially those on regular lines between Mediterranean and British ports, never approached the Spanish coast.

The Danish motor vessels *Thyra S* and *Torfinn Jarl* were both stopped in the Straits and taken to Ceuta under force of arms, but following inspection were allowed to leave.

The steamer *Menin Ridge* refused to submit to a Nationalist Armed Trawler which fired on her in the Straits of Gibraltar on March 23, 1937. *(Welsh Industrial & Maritime Museum)*

On March 23 the steamer *Menin Ridge* owned by the single-ship company, the Ridge Steamship Co. Ltd., of Phoenix Buildings, Mount Stuart Square, Cardiff, which was carrying a cargo of coal from Barry to Oran was approached in the Straits of Gibraltar by an armed insurgent trawler which ordered her to stop, and fired a shot across the merchant ships bow. Captain Powell of Rumney Hill, Cardiff, master of the *Menin Ridge* refused to comply and maintained his course and speed, and eventually the armed trawler left when a French destroyer appeared on the scene. In a letter home Captain Powell gave the following account:

> While passing through the Straits of Gibraltar I was signalled to by a Spanish Armed Trawler who demanded to know our destination and then he ordered me to stop, or he would open fire. I disregarded both orders and maintained my course and speed. He fired a warning shot, but shortly afterwards a French destroyer came along and the trawler turned back. I reported the matter to the Admiralty at Gibraltar and shortly afterwards HMS *Garland* caught us up and was given particulars of the incident. Our position at the time was 5 miles 330 degrees from Almina Point and outside Territorial Waters.

Also in March the *Stanholme* owned by J.A. Billmeir's Stanhope Steamship Co. Ltd., of London, was loading at Casablanca, North Africa, for Spain, and the Nationalists made a formal complaint to the British Authorities at Gibraltar to the effect that she was indeed loading war contraband. The British Consul at Casablanca made an immediate investigation, and satisfied himself that the charge was unfounded. However, the Nationalists were not satisfied with this, and intercepted the *Stanholme* outside territorial waters and escorted her under force of arms to Gibraltar, where the authorities again carefully scrutinised her papers and cargo at a cost of a 24 hour delay to the vessel.

Resulting out of this incident, and those concerning the *Springwear* and *Menin Ridge*, the British Naval Commander-in-Chief in the Mediterranean, Admiral Sir A. Dudley Pound sent a protest to the Spanish Nationalist

Naval Authorities at Cadiz.

On March 25 a Nationalist squadron of three Junker and four Fiat aircraft made a fierce attack on a number of merchant ships lying in port at Musel, near Gijon, on the North Coast, twelve or fourteen bombs were dropped, their chief objective appeared to be the Bilbao registered *Itxas Ondo*. One bomb struck the ship's bridge blowing it into the sea. The master disappeared in the waves and a number of other sailors were wounded. The aircraft then swooped down and raked the decks with machine-gun fire.

On the same day in the South, the Spanish motor vessel *Araya Mendi* in ballast from Valencia put into Algiers with fire and bomb damage from an air attack. She was allowed to stay to effect temporary repairs.

A day later the French liner *Imerethir II* was stopped by an insurgent cruiser, believed to be the *Canarias* 50 miles North-east of Alicante. She had on board 430 refugees from Valencia and Alicante bound for Marseilles. She wirelessed her position to the French warship *Suffren* which ordered her to stay in her present position. When the insurgent cruiser was told of the impending arrival of the French warship, the vessel withdrew, and thereafter with the arrival of the *Suffren* the liner was escorted for the remainder of the voyage.

On March 28 the London registered steamer *Magdalena* which was carrying a cargo of minerals from La Goulette, Tunisia for Bayonne (France) was fired on by an insurgent warship when 20 miles off Santander. The warship fired six shells across the merchant ships bows whereupon she stopped and after being examined by the insurgent was allowed to proceed. The *Magdalena* was owned by the Lensen Company of London and was commanded by Captain James Thompson of St. Michaels Road, Llandaff, Cardiff, who was accompanied on board by his 17 year old son Peter, who was a pupil at Cardiff High School.

A day later the Spanish steamer *Mar Caspio* with a cargo of 2,000 tons of coal from Newcastle for Bayonne was attacked and shelled by two insurgent warships while she was in French territorial waters off Cape Breton, 10 miles North of Bayonne. 15 shells were fired at the merchant ship and she was hit at the waterline. In an attempt to save his ship the master ran aground on the bar of the River Adour, where she was to become a total loss.

The French steamer *Cap Falcon* was hailed by an insurgent patrol boat when 15 miles off Santander. One shell was fired but the merchant ship was not struck. She was soon allowed to proceed.

At the same time the Danish steamer *Jutta* was seized in the Straits and taken to Ceuta.

An incident involving the London registered *Thorpehall* took place on March 30, 1937. This ship was owned by the Westcliffe Steamship Co. Ltd., of London, a company formed on October 23, 1936 specifically to carry cargo for the Republican Government. Of its 1,000 shares 499 each were held by two Greek Nationals, Messrs Basil Pandelis and John Katepodis, whilst a mere two shares were held by the company secretary Gordon Till who was in fact a British subject. Therefore this was a company, as pointed out by Franco, that was set up to take advantage of the Spanish situation by principally foreign nationals to get the benefit of British Naval protection.

The *Thorpehall* under the command of Capt. Joseph Andrews was on a voyage from Valencia for Bilbao and had called at Gibraltar for bunkers and having just left this port was signalled to stop by the Nationalist gunboat *Eduardo Dato*. Captain Andrews ignored this instruction and immediately altered course and brought his vessel back to Gibraltar. On the following morning the ship was escorted out of Gibraltar by HMS *Gypsey* and having passed through the Straits carried on her voyage alone. But as I will show in the next chapter the Nationalists did not give up.

## Chapter 4

# THE BLOCKADE OF BILBAO

The situation in Spain in early 1937 had seen Malaga fall to the Nationalists in the South, but a stalemate existed at Madrid. Franco's troops had reached the gates of Madrid but could get no further, and as a result the Republican slogan 'they shall not pass' was changed to the more appropriate 'they cannot pass'. The successful defence of Madrid had caused the Nationalists to delay their offensive in the North, however, early in April the great push began.

There had been considerable Nationalist naval activity in the North over the past weeks, and a number of ships had been captured or sunk. The Panamanian flag *Andra* chartered to the Cardiff firm of Emlyn-Jones, Griffin and Co. Ltd., whilst making for Bilbao was on April 5 intercepted by the Nationalist cruiser *Almirante Cervera* in thick fog, shelled and sunk.

Meanwhile the *Thorpehall* with her cargo of food was some eight miles off the North Spanish coast on April 6 when she was intercepted by the cruiser *Almirante Cervera* and the armed trawler *Galerna* which fired a shell across her bow. The merchant ship stopped but immediately sent out a distress message which was answered by three British destroyers, the *Brazen, Blanche* and *Beagle*. The British Consul at Bilbao was on board HMS *Blanche* and using a megaphone asked the Nationalists what they thought they were doing. The Spanish persisted in their view that they had captured the *Thorpehall* and as a result the *Blanche* and *Beagle* prepared for action whilst the *Brazen* escorted the merchant ship to the three mile limit off Bilbao. Thereafter the Spanish warships sailed away, showing a disinclination to quarrel with the Royal Navy.

On the same day, April 6, General Franco announced that he would stop all ships from entering ports in Northern Spain, and set about stopping food getting to the Basques. There was already a shortage of food in the Northern territory and news of this blockade came as a considerable blow to the Basques.

The Blockade of Bilbao caused a storm in Britain, where public opinion was firmly on the side of the Republicans and Basques. The political ramifications of the blockade are dealt with at length by Hugh Thomas in his book *The Spanish Civil War* which I can do no better than quote.

> The announcement of this blockade placed the British Government in a difficult position. By international law, a blockade (including the right of search on the high seas) could be carried out by belligerents in war. But specifically because they did not wish to subject British merchantmen to the search of Spanish naval vessels, Baldwin and his Ministers were opposed to the recognition of the two Spanish warring parties as belligerents. Nearly all British trade with Spain was now carried on with Republican ports. But the Nationalists had command of the seas. Therefore, if belligerent rights were granted, it would be mainly Nationalist naval vessels that would be doing the intercepting and mainly British merchant men which would suffer. But here was a blockade declared of Northern Spanish ports. Unless belligerent rights were admitted, British merchant ships would be entitled to ask for the aid of the Royal Navy if they were interfered with outside the Basque Territorial waters of three miles from the shore. How much less trouble, therefore, it would be if there were no British merchant ships going to Basque ports at all.

> This last reflection, perhaps made only subconsciously, no doubt disposed the British Admiralty to believe certain new reports. The captain of HMS *Blanche* bluntly signalled that the Nationalist blockade was effective. Sir Henry Chilton reported the same from Hendaye. There were other similar naval reports; not only was a Spanish Nationalist naval group outside Bilbao in a position to prevent the entry of all merchantmen; but the Basque territorial waters were mined. Thus (reported Chiltern and the Navy) it would be actually dangerous for British merchant ships to try and enter Bilbao. Inside the three-mile limit, of course, the Royal Navy had no right to protect merchantmen. And since the Basques had obviously lost command of the sea, attacks might well be carried out against British ships within the territorial waters. So on April 8 the Admiralty instructed all British

merchant vessels within a hundred miles of Bilbao to repair to the French fishing port and resort of St. Jean de Luz, and to await further orders. The following day, Sir Henry Chiltern was told by Troncoso, the Nationalist Military Governor of Irun, on instructions from Burgos, that Franco was determined to make the blockade effective. The voyage of four British merchantmen known to be bearing food cargoes and now at St. Jean de Luz would in particular be prevented by force. Meantime, more mines would be laid across Bilbao harbour. This determined statement reached London on the morning of Saturday April 10. It caused Mr Baldwin to summon the Cabinet for Sunday. Back from their week-ends came among others Mr. Duff Cooper, Secretary of State for War, Sir Samuel Hoare, the First Lord of the Admiralty, Sir John Simon, the Home Secretary, and Mr. Eden, the Foreign Secretary. As a result of the Cabinet, the Board of Trade 'warned' British ships not to go to Bilbao, and intimated that the Navy could not help them if they tried to do so, Mr. Baldwin explained this decision to an angry House of Commons on the Monday. There were risks, he said, against which it was impossible to protect British Shipping.

Throughout the following week there was mounting uproar in Parliament. All that spring Spain had been an incessant topic for question-time and for debates on foreign affairs. Eden and Cranborne, the Foreign Secretary and his Lieutenant, had been hard pressed both by Labour and Liberal sympathisers for the Republic and by the handful of Conservatives who supported the Nationalists. Had the Government heard of the arrival of new Italian divisions at Cadiz? How many Russians were there at Madrid? How many British volunteers had been killed while fighting with the International Brigades? To most of these questions, the Government, concerned above all to maintain and develop non-intervention, had always professed ignorance of exact information. Now the interest of the House of Commons in the cause of Spain reached a climax. On April 14, Mr. Attlee for the Labour Party moved a vote of censure. The British Government, the greatest maritime power in the world, had given up trying to protect British shipping; yet the Basque President had said that the mines in Bilbao harbour had been cleared, that at night armed trawlers (aided by searchlights) protected the port. Where did the Government gain its information of the dangers? Did it do so from 'those curious people, our consular agents, who seem so silent on the question of Italian troops landing?' Sir John Simon, the Home Secretary, next argued that if British ships were to be allowed to go to Bilbao, there would have to be mine-sweeping. That would constitute intervention in favour of the Republic. Sir Archibald Sinclair, the Liberal Leader, argued that the Government's acceptance of the Nationalist blockade spelled intervention. The Germans, after all, he said, recalling incidents of the winter, had always looked after *their* ships. Mr. Churchill spoke next. he reiterated his Olympian detachment for either side in the war and indulged in a day-dream of mediation through 'some meeting in what Lord Rosebery once called a "wayside inn" which would give the chance in Spain of peace, of law, of bread and of oblivion'. Then indeed these 'clenched fists might relax into the open hands of generous co-operation'. Mr. Harold Nicolson described the refusal to risk British ships in Basque waters as a bitter pill. It is not pleasant. It is a potion which is almost nauseating', but it had to be accepted. Mr. Duncan Sandys urged the grant of belligerent rights, as only then could one expect the two sides to obey the rules of war. Mr. Noel Baker recalled that it was the first time since 1588 that the British had been afraid of the Spanish fleet. Mr. Eden ended the debate (which was of course won by the Government) by saying that if British merchant ships did leave St. Jean de Luz, and so disobeyed the Board of Trade warning, they would be given naval protection as far as the three-mile limit. 'Our hope is that they will not go because in view of reports of conditions we do not think it safe for them to go'.

*Copyright – Hugh Thomas 1961.*

Whilst all this was going on in Britain those British merchant ships within 100 miles of Bilbao were carrying out the instruction given by the Board of Trade. The first ship arrived at St. Jean de Luz on April 8 and by the following day there were four vessels at anchor awaiting orders (and developments). It was here that the legend of 'Potato' Jones was made. Of these four ships three were Welsh owned. The *Marie Llewellyn* managed by Claude Angel of Cardiff, and commanded by Captain David John Jones of Waterloo Place, Swansea, was loaded with potatoes destined for Santander, although it has been suggested that this cargo actually concealed arms. Her voyage had commenced at Antwerp. Captain Owen Jones who lived at 16, Victoria Avenue, Canton, Cardiff, commanded the Guardian Line's

*Macgregor* which had a general cargo consisting mainly of foodstuffs and grain. The Llanelli registered *Sarastone* with a cargo of foodstuffs, mainly potatoes and grain from Antwerp, was also commanded by a Captain Jones. The fourth steamer was the Newcastle owned *Hamsterley* loaded with foodstuffs also and commanded by a Captain Still. The fact that three of the masters were named Jones prompted the international press to nickname them, and thereafter they became 'Potato' Jones (*Marie Llewellyn*), 'Corn Cob' Jones (*Macgregor*) and 'Ham and Egg' Jones (*Sarastone*).

Interest in the situation at St. Jean de Luz was widespread and was fuelled by the pretended sailings of one or more of the ships, and the statements of some of the masters particularly 'Potato' Jones who will be remembered in history for his part, deserved or not.

A fifth ship to arrive off Northern Spain since the blockade was declared was the Cardiff steamer *Seven Seas Spray* which was commanded by Captain William H. Roberts, a Cornishman who had previously lived at Penarth, but was now resident at Okehampton, Devon. This ship was on route from Alicante with a general cargo which consisted of drums of olive oil, tinned foods, salt, barrels of wine, cognac, hams, horse fodder and other foods. The master was accompanied by his nineteen year old daughter Florence, and the Chief Engineer's wife Mrs. B. Docker was also on board. When off the North Spanish coast she was hailed by HMS *Blanche* who directed her not to attempt to enter Bilbao, her intended destination, but to make for St. Jean de Luz instead. The *Seven Seas Spray* was well outside Spanish territorial waters, and I believe that it was Captain Robert's intention to actually defy the instruction from the Board of Trade which had been reinforced by the British destroyer, and when parallel with Bilbao was going to alter course and enter the port. However, it is plain that the Nationalists also realised this, as the cruiser *Almirante Cervera* met her on April 10 as she made her way along the Basque coast and accompanied her past Bilbao, thus ensuring that she did not enter. The ship arrived at St. Jean de Luz the following day.

On the evening of April 11 the *Macgregor* sailed from St. Jean de Luz and later arrived at Bayonne where she awaited further orders.

Previously the Royal Navy had only kept a small destroyer force on patrol in the Bay of Biscay, but this had been increased to up to four destroyers and was subsequently reinforced by a battleship, HMS *Royal Oak* and a cruiser HMS *Hood* which were based on St. Jean de Luz. Other nations had naval forces off the North Spanish coast including Germany and France.

At this time the Board of Trade reinforced their instructions to shipowners as follows:–

> The Board of Trade desires merchant vessels not to enter Basque ports for the time being on account of the dangerous conditions. We request that instructions be given that vessels should remain at St. Jean de Luz or some other French port, awaiting instructions and co-operating with the Naval Authorities.

On April 12 the Prime Minister, Mr. Baldwin made the following statement giving the British Government's attitude in respect of British Shipping trading to ports in the vicinity of the Spanish War zone:–

> His Majesty's Government cannot recognise or concede belligerent rights and they cannot tolerate any interference with British Shipping at sea. They are, however, warning British shipping that, in view of conditions at present prevailing in the neighbourhood of Bilbao, they should not, for practical reasons, and in view of the risks against which it is at present impossible to protect them, go into that area so long as the conditions prevail. The Vice-Admiral commanding Battle Cruiser Squadron in HMS *Hood* has been sent to the North Coast of Spain.

On this date the Consett Iron Company's steamer *Leadgate* arrived at Bayonne where she joined the *Macgregor*. The *Leadgate*, although registered at Newcastle, had previously been a unit of Walter Vaughan's fleet managed from Cory Buildings, Mount Stuart Square, Cardiff, and had until a few months earlier been named *Seven Seas Sound*. The ships awaiting orders at this time at St. Jean de Luz were the *Marie Llewellyn, Sarastone, Seven Seas Spray* and *Hamsterley*. At this time Captain 'Potato' Jones started to voice concern about the condition of his cargo of potatoes which he stated was going bad.

Potato Jones publically voiced his opinion of the Nationalist Navy – 'Spanish Navy? Never heard of it since the Armada'. His view of the situation off Northern Spain was similarly flippant. 'It makes me sick, thinking of these Spanish Dons strutting about the quarter-decks of their miserable ships intimidating the British Navy and interfering with shipping'. His words endeared him to the British public, and he quickly became regarded as a hero, particularly in his native Swansea. However, the British Government and Royal Navy were less pleased.

At this time the world's attention was focused on St. Jean de Luz, and speculation was rife as to the various masters' intentions. The Royal Navy had instructions to go to the assistance of British merchant ships if summoned, but not to convoy vessels. At this time Captain Still of the *Hamsterley* expressed his willingness to proceed and accompany other vessels, as his ship was fitted with wireless, while others such as 'Potato' Jones's *Marie Llewellyn* was not. The owner of this ship did not allow him to carry out his offer, or certainly not at that stage.

A spokesman for Stone and Rolfe Ltd., of Llanelli, when asked their intention regarding the *Sarastone* said, 'It was on Admiralty advice that she put into port and it will be on their advice that she leaves'. A similar statement was made by the Consett Iron Company regarding their *Leadgate* which was actually in ballast and had been destined to load a cargo of iron ore at Bilbao. On April 14 a spokesman for the Guardian Line dismissed reports that Captain 'Corn Cob' Jones had asked for permission to try to run the blockade, as 'utter nonsense'. But it is interesting to note that on that day the manager Alan Roberts was unavailable for comment as he was in London attending a meeting of the Chamber of Shipping called to discuss the situation.

The Sunderland registered steamer *Brinkburn* succeeded in leaving Bilbao on April 14, 1937 with a cargo of iron ore.
*(John Clarkson)*

On April 15 the Stone & Rolfe steamer *Sarastone* was ordered to Bordeaux by the French Authorities for her cargo to be examined.

*(Welsh Industrial & Maritime Museum)*

The steamer *Marie Llewellyn*. *(Laurence Dunn Collection)*

On Thursday, April 15 after two days steaming outside, due to heavy weather preventing her from docking, the steamer *Magdelena* entered St. Jean de Luz and anchored. It was announced that the Sunderland registered steamer *Brinkburn* had successfully left Bilbao on April 14 with a cargo of iron ore, and in the following days a small number of ships managed to leave Bilbao. However, these ships had been in port prior to the declaration by the Nationalists of the blockade, and it was more the intention of stopping ships entering that they were interested in. This announcement may have influenced some of the masters at St. Jean de Luz and Bayonne, as a number were openly stating that they felt the effectiveness of the blockade was vastly exaggerated and they doubted that Bilbao was mined.

At 3pm on April 15 the *Sarastone* sailed from St. Jean de Luz having been ordered by the French Authorities to proceed to Bordeaux for her cargo to be examined.

At 4pm suddenly and without warning the *Marie Llewellyn* weighed anchor and without permission from or informing the harbour master, she set sail from the port. She was observed to be heading on the same course as the *Sarastone* initially, but after an hour or so it was noted from the shore that she was changing course until when she finally disappeared from sight she was facing in the direction of the Spanish coast, and was pitching heavily in the big swell which was running.

Speculation in the world press was aroused by the now famous Captain 'Potato' Jones, who had previously to the blockade been known as 'Swansea' Jones, by the American press was referred to as 'Casey' Jones, and by the Spanish Republicans as Jones 'el Patatero'. The *Times* correspondent wrote, 'Potato Jones confided his intentions to no one before sailing, but it may be that the honour of being first to run the blockade will fall to him'. However it was not to be, as darkness fell he was stopped by a British destroyer and turned back, returning to St. Jean de Luz on the following morning. Apparently lurking in the distance ahead of him was a Nationalist vessel which would have intercepted him but for the timely intervention of the Royal Navy. I particularly like the account of this affair given in the *Times*:–

"Potato" Jones, skipper of the *Marie Llewellyn* is an angry man. His attempt to run through General Franco's blockade to a Spanish port – probably Gijon – has failed. After a night spent in battling with a heavy swell the *Marie Llewellyn* crept into here (St. Jean de Luz) this morning a crestfallen ship. Under cover of darkness and dazzling rain, she might have slipped past the Nationalist warships with luck on her side. But the skipper forgot perhaps, that General Franco's warships are not the only watchers on the coast of Spain, and that other high authorities besides those of Salamanca disapprove of blockade running.

It was not a Spanish Cruiser, but a British Destroyer that loomed up alongside the *Marie Llewellyn* at midnight and put an end to her wanderings. It was English not in Spanish that "advice" of a kind which could not well be disregarded was winked by flashlight or bawled through a megaphone to her. "Potato" Jones does not admit all this, or, indeed, any of it, to inquisitive Journalists.

It is not the least of his sufferings that having failed in his venture, he cannot even divulge in the relief of telling his story. Some mysterious power, emanating by unknown channels from His Majesty's Navy, has struck him dumb. It has done more than that. Not content with silence, it has enlisted his powers of imagination against himself, and "Potato" Jones's powers of imagination are remarkable. The yarn which he spun on his return to harbour combined true ingenuity and apparent bluffness in exquisite proportions. It would be convincing as well as diverting if other sources of truth were not available for its author's undoing.

When I scrambled on board the *Marie Llewellyn* this morning over bulwarks – thoughtfully coated with fresh paint for the convenience of visitors an air of mystery hung over the crew. The seaman who made my boat fast had been pleasantly talkative on Wednesday. Today he would only grin when asked if the voyage had been a success, the mate's description of the night's escapade was a nod and the words, 'not so bad', murmured with eyes fixed on the dim Spanish mountains. The intelligent steward, polishing the brass rail on the saloon mantelpiece with a nice blend of domestic devotion and sailorly happiness, remarked brightly that there were too many warships about in these waters. The captain, he added, was having a wash.

On my first visit to the *Marie Llewellyn*, "Potato" Jones, roused from his afternoon nap, had tumbled out of his bunk in his shirt and reached for his trousers with good-humoured tolerance. He now emerged from his bathroom in trousers, only with a light in his eye. Towelling his topsides aggressively, he got his blow in first.

"What do you want?" he demanded – a disabling question – and without waiting for an answer he plunged into the public version of his adventures. "The Spanish coast", he exploded, "Why should I go to the Spanish coast". I can't go there, can I? I can't go against Admiralty orders".

Captain David John 'Potato' Jones master of the *Marie Llewellyn* who attempted to break the Blockade of Bilbao on the night of April 15/16, 1937. *(Western Mail)*

A flash, pure mischief, drove the wrath from his face. "Where the Navy won't go I can't go either, can I; that's fair, isn't it; yes or no? You want to know where I went", he said, "Well this ship's short of water; I went to Bayonne to get water, and that's all there is to it. I've got to get fresh water somewhere, haven't I? There's no water-boat here. At St. Jean de Luz I'm offering £5 to anyone who puts it on board; £5 a ton and no takers. 4/- a ton is what I paid at Bayonne. We can't get on without fresh water, can we. So I says to myself yesterday, 'I'm going to Bayonne for water; I'll get into Bayonne by hook or by crook, bar or no bar'. But you know what the weather's been like for two or three days. I tried the bar, and I couldn't get through. Two or three times I tried, but with a big swell running you can't get the bar at Bayonne. It's the most dangerous place in the world to get into. Last time I came out over the bar in rough weather I felt the bottom would drop out of the ship the way she barged down on the water after leaping the swell. You saw me turn West you say? Bayonne does not lie West from here. Did you see me pitching? I had to run head to sea to open water before I could turn'.

"Potato" Jones glared fiercely, driving home his words. Livid, but loyal, he swallowed his anger, improving on the silence which had been recommended to him. It seemed unkind to ask awkward questions – why, for instance, should a captain of his experience try to get into Bayonne at night when the place was so dangerous, and everyone knew that the bar was impassable? Followed by the pitying gaze of the steward, we went over the side and ashore together without further reference to the adventures of the *Marie Llewellyn.*

The true story was a little different from Potato Jones's genial romance. It oozed out from various sources during the day. By sailing without notice or permission from St. Jean de Luz and heading boldly for Spain "Potato" Jones had plunged into a complex of forces of which he was blissfully ignorant. To begin with, so long as he was outside Spanish territorial waters he was entitled to protection by the Royal Navy against the very real perils which might beset him. But he had no wireless and his ship was a tiny object for the one British destroyer on patrol to locate. Worst of all, the minefields of Bilbao and Santander – already objects of scepticism to all the British captains – were not, as he imagined, the only dangers in his path. As he ploughed his way Westwards through the gathering darkness his course was leading him straight into the jaws of the battleship *Espana,* which, unknown to him, but well known to the British destroyer, was cruising in his path. By great good luck HMS *Brazen* found the *Marie Llewellyn* and hailed her in time.

Details of the meeting are lacking, but it may safely be supposed that wicked words or their equivalent in electric flashes sped for a time over the deep. Whatever was said "Potato" Jones found the Navy's advice to go home convincing, and added to it a chastened desire to say nothing of his experience.

As for the Navy, it is entitled to consider that it had done its duty by the *Marie Llewellyn* if the rescue of venturesome sailors from the consequences of their temerity may be regarded as a branch of Naval protection.

Back in Cardiff, the ship's manager Claude Angel was giving nothing away. In interviews given to the press he stated that he had no information regarding the *Marie Llewellyn's* attempt to break the blockade, and that if it were true he would have been the first to know. Similarly, "Potato" Jones's daughter Mrs B. Chappell, with whom he lived when at home at Waterloo Place, Swansea, said that when her father was away at sea she rarely heard from him. What she knew of his movements were those she had read in the newspapers. Of her father she said, "He believes in the maxim that if anything happens to him we will hear soon enough", she added, "It is a very anxious time for us, but I suppose he knows what he is about. He is just the sort of man who would do such a thing. He likes adventures and fears nobody". This lady obviously knew her father very well.

Captain David John "Potato" Jones was a well known figure in South Wales shipping circles. He was in fact a part owner of the Dillwyn Steamship Co. Ltd., which owned the ship. Prior to 1924 he had commanded vessels owned by Owen and Watkin Williams and Company of Cardiff. After that he sailed with a number of local shipowners and subsequently retired from the sea. However, after a short period ashore he went back to sea and joined the firm of Claude Angel and Co. Ltd., and had previously commanded their steamer *Bramhill* which had already been involved in an incident with the Nationalist Navy.

However, on Saturday April 17 Potato Jones gave up his attempt to break the Nationalist blockade and set sail for Alicante with his ruined cargo of potatoes. Before he left he answered journalists questions as to his destination with the blunt "Avonmouth". So even after the *Marie Llewellyn* left nobody was sure whether he had really given up the attempt. Historians over the years have actually credited him with breaking the blockade in Northern Spain at that time, but this is definitely not so. The ship arrived at Gibraltar for bunkers on April 23 en route for Alicante where she was to

'Potato' Jones at St. Jean de Luz. *(Western Mail)*

The *Marie Llewllyn* gave up her attempt to break the blockade, and sailed for Alicante on April 17.

*(John Clarkson)*

load a cargo of fruit for Antwerp. Meanwhile Claude Angel's steamer *Bramhill* had left Valencia on April 15 on passage for the North coast with a cargo of foodstuffs destined for Bilbao. When asked if this was correct Claude Angel would only say that 'it is far too dangerous for the ship to attempt to enter Bilbao'.

On April 17, in view of the situation off Northern Spain the Chamber of Shipping of the United Kingdom issued advice on the wording of charter parties to be entered into by shipowners contemplating using their ships on voyages to ports affected by the Spanish Civil War. The advice was very comprehensive and is of such interest that I have reproduced it in full.

The Master shall not be required or bound to sign bills of lading for any blockaded port or for any port which the master or owners in his or their discretion consider dangerous or impossible to reach.

If any port of discharge be blockaded, or if, owing to any war hostilities, warlike operations, civil war, civil commotions, revolutions, or the operation of international law; entry to any such port or discharge of cargo intended for any such port be considered by the master or owners in his or their discretion dangerous or prohibited, or

It is considered by the master or owners in his or their discretion dangerous or impossible for the vessel to reach such discharging port.

The cargo, or such part of it as may be affected, shall be discharged at any safe port in the vicinity of the said port of discharge as may be ordered by the charterers.

If no such orders be received from the charterers within 48 hours after they, or their agents, have received from the owners a request for the nomination of a substitute discharging port, the owners shall then be at liberty to discharge the cargo at any safe port which they or the master may in their or his discretion decide on, and such discharge shall be deemed to be due fulfilment of the contract or contracts of affreightment so far as cargo so discharged is concerned.

In the event of cargo being discharged at any such other port the owners shall be entitled to freight as if the discharge had been effected at the port or ports originally designated or to which the vessel may have been ordered pursuant to the terms of the bills of lading.

The vessel shall have liberty to comply with any directions or recommendations as to departure, arrival, routes, ports of call, stoppages, destination, zones, waters, delivery or in any other wise whatsoever given by the Government of the nation under whose flag the vessel sails, or any other Government or local authority, including any *de facto* Government or authority or by any committee or person having, under the terms of the war risks insurance on the vessel, the right to give any such directions or recommendations.

If by reason of or in compliance with any such directions or recommendations the vessel does not proceed to the port or ports originally designated or to which she may have been ordered pursuant to the terms of the bills of lading, the vessel may proceed to any safe port which the master or owners in his or their discretion may decide on and there discharge the cargo.

Such cargo shall be deemed to be due fulfilment of the contract or contracts of affreightment and the owners shall be entitled to freight as if discharge had been effected at the port or ports originally designated or to which the vessel may have been ordered pursuant to the terms of the bills of lading.

The effect of the above being included in charter parties was to ensure payment for the shipowner whatever happened to the cargo or whoever interfered with the passage of the vessel. Payment was due even if the ship was captured and the cargo seized. The trade was not without its risks. The vessels were insured for war risks in addition to their normal policies, and crew insurance was also paid. In addition, after some early disputes with crews, a 50% war bonus over and above their normal wages was paid to the seamen 24 hours before arrival in the Spanish War zone until 24 hours after leaving the zone.

Such was the plight of the people of Northern Spain with near starvation rations, that following the failure of Potato Jones to break through with his cargo, the Basque Government addressed themselves to the masters of the ships awaiting orders and developments at St. Jean de Luz and Bayonne. The offer of special bonuses was made. The sum of 5,000 francs (£50) each was on offer if they left on Saturday April 17, 4,000 francs was offered if they left on the Sunday, and so on, decreasing by 1,000 francs for each day of waiting. The cargoes were urgently needed, and the attention and sympathy of most of the world was focused on the starving people of Bilbao (and other areas of Northern Spain).

The Basques gave assurances that adequate protection could be given to merchantmen within the three mile limit off Bilbao and that there were no danger from mines as the entrance of the port had been swept. They cited the London steamer *Thorpehall* as an example. This ship had entered Bilbao on April 6 and succeeded in leaving and skirting the coast to enter Gijon in the West on April 19. However the owners of the vessel on realising this, had given orders for Captain Andrews to sail at once for La Pallice (France) and to place himself under the instructions of the Royal Navy, which he complied with. The steamer *Leadgate* which had been at Bayonne had been ordered by her owners to proceed to Brest and subsequently directed that she give up her attempt to enter Bilbao and directed her back to Sunderland.

On April 19 the Welsh steamer *Sarastone* commanded by Captain 'Ham and Egg' Jones arrived at Bordeaux at the instructions of the French authorities. The non-intervention committee was due to come into force at 12 midnight on that date, and the ship was suspected of carrying war materials. There was considerable support and sympathy in France for the Basque cause and as a result the dockers refused to unload the ship to allow the inspection to be carried out. The dockers had originally consented to unload that part of the cargo which consisted of decaying foodstuffs, but on realising that the Non-Intervention Control Officers were going to take advantage of this to more closely inspect the whole cargo immediately walked off the ship. Whilst the majority of the cargo consisted of foodstuffs, there was a consignment of nickel coins on board which it was feared by the control officers would finish up in the Basque factories to help in the manufacture of munitions. Therefore they declared the coins as war material. After a week or two the French Trade Union movement allowed the resumption of work by the dockers and after the removal of the offending cargo, and that part of the foodstuffs which had decayed, she was allowed to leave.

At this time, in view of "Potato" Jones abandoning his attempt to break the blockade, it was felt that none of the other masters at either St. Jean de Luz or Bayonne would be likely to attempt the run. Indeed when asked by a reporter from the *Western Mail* on Sunday April 18, Alfred Pope, the owner of the *Seven Seas Spray* said that it was foolish in his opinion, for any ship to attempt to run the blockade. He had been in contact with London, Paris and St. Jean de Luz and it was not likely that any vessel would try, especially in view of the new Board of Trade instructions. The *Seven Seas Spray* was still at St. Jean de Luz he said, but he expected news regarding her next move within the next 24 hours.

Alfred Pope's *Seven Seas Spray* which broke the Blockade of Bilbao on April 20, 1937.          (*F. W. Hawks*)

Alfred Pope was actually saying what the British Government and General Franco wanted to hear. The Nationalist Naval forces off North Spain were now confident that none of the ships would attempt to break the blockade, particularly in view of the failure of 'Potato' Jones to get through. This view was also held by the Royal Navy. However, Alfred Pope had sent his partner Thomas McEwen to St. Jean de Luz when he heard that the ship had arrived on April 11 to discuss the situation with the master. Alfred Pope had no intentions of giving up the attempt to break into Bilbao, but as a shrewd man kept his intentions to himself. There was nothing to be gained, but plenty to be lost by declaring his intentions to General Franco's forces.

On the night of Monday 19th at about 10pm the Cardiff registered steamer *Seven Seas Spray* weighed anchor at St. Jean de Luz and got under way with the intention of attempting to break the blockade. She had not requested permission from the harbour master to leave and had not informed anyone of the intention to go. As those ashore became aware of the departure of the ship they signalled to her to stop, but Captain Roberts ignored them. The ship had no sooner left the port than she sighted a man-of-war which passed her close by. The *Seven Seas Spray* was not displaying any navigation lights, and fortunately the warship did not see her, as it was confirmed that it must have been a Nationalist vessel. As the Welsh merchant ship steamed on her way towards the Spanish coast she was approached by a British destroyer ten miles off the coast which signalled to her, "Where bound?" to which the *Seven Seas Spray* replied "Bilbao". The destroyer warned Captain Roberts that he entered at his own risk, which he accepted, and then wished him good luck. Thereafter the valiant Welsh ship with her valuable and much needed cargo of food continued her voyage towards the Basque port. On arrival in the river she was met by Basque warships and aircraft overhead, and was escorted into the port in triumphant fashion. It was a most moving occasion to those on board the ship, as tens of thousand of inhabitants of Bilbao thronged the river banks to greet them. Captain Roberts and his daughter on the bridge of the ship were almost overcome by this reception and open display of gratitude. Hungry people in the crowds, men, women and children, saluted them and shouted, 'Long live the British sailors, Long Live Liberty.'

The Basque Government were so grateful for the efforts made by the ship to enter Bilbao that the Ministers of Finance, Commerce and Supply entertained Captain Roberts, his daughter and Thomas McEwen at a dinner in their honour. Captain Roberts was presented with a silver cigarette case embossed with the Basque flag and with an inscription expressing the thanks of the Basque people, while his daughter was given a bracelet.

Captain W.H. Roberts and his daughter entertained to a dinner in their honour by Basque Ministers following their successful entry into Bilbao.

(*Western Mail*)

On hearing of the successful entry of his ship into Bilbao Alfred Pope told newsmen:–

I knew it could be done. My steamer has shown that Franco's blockade is nothing but boast and tommy rot. A British steamer has opened the way for shipping. I hope that the 'Spray* has blazed a trail and shown the rest of the vessels in St. Jean de Luz the way home to Bilbao. She had not the slightest difficulty in carrying her cargo of 4,000 tons of foodstuffs into the port.

She left Alicante some time last week but off Bilbao was told by the Navy that it was dangerous to make for that port. The master, Captain Roberts, made for St. Jean de Luz and communicated with us. Mr. McEwen left immediately for St. Jean de Luz and arrived there on Sunday. He had a talk with the master and members of the crew and thoroughly examined every angle of the situation. Captain Roberts is a Cornishman. Mr. McEwen had a talk with him and the crew about the proposition. They were quite agreeable. "Let's go" was their answer to him.

In the meantime I spoke to the insurance people, and they told me that I was not covered if the 'Spray* made for Bilbao. However we agreed to take the risk ourselves, and last night the 'Spray* put out in the darkness for Bilbao. Actually she was only a little way out when an Insurgent warship passed her, but in the darkness could not have recognised her as the ship which was escorted past Bilbao earlier in the week by a rebel cruiser.

I think we have shown up the silly statements made by Franco and his men. Bilbao is wide open, and as long as we get cargoes we shall take them in, whatever the British Navy says or whatever it fails to do for us. A blockade is all tommy rot. After all, we are in business, and considerations for the starving people of the Basque country apart, we had to remember that we had a cargo which might turn rotten on us and be a dead loss

The Basque Government now tell me that everything is all right and that the way is safe for shipping. My partner and the Captain did the trick themselves. We were determined to get in and we got in. We hope that other people will get in as well. We have been trading to Spain for a long time and never once during this have our ships failed to get where they were chartered for; and if it is humanly possible they never will fail.

Blockade or no blockade General Franco is not going to keep a single one of our ships from going about its lawful occasions. I was certain that what the Basque Government told me was right. I have been dealing with them since the start, and I have never known them tell me anything which

Captain W.H. Roberts, master of the *Seven Seas Spray.*
(*Western Mail*)

Alfred Pope, owner of the *Seven Seas Spray.*
(*Western Mail*)

was untrue. I have not yet decided on the *Seven Seas Spray's* next port of call. That will depend on circumstances.

Captain Roberts sent his account of the adventure to the *Western Mail* in a long telegram.

Left St. Jean de Luz last night at 10 o'clock after eight days stay. We came out of port and steamed all night without any incidents whatsoever, arriving here at 8am, and receiving an escort of trawlers, battleships, and aeroplanes (in the entry channel only); also covered by shore batteries, which I considered were under the circumstances unnecessary, as no mines or rebel warships were in evidence at daylight. We were challenged by a British destroyer, who asked "Where bound?". Replied "Bilbao". I was informed that I entered at my own risk, which I accepted. Was then wished good luck. The destroyer at St. Jean de Luz had previously said that we would not be able to enter Bilbao and would only have protection whilst outside the three mile limit. (A reference to warning to all merchantmen at the French port). Nevertheless we did it, and it was worth it to receive the great ovation all along both sides of the river from all the people and children. The passage was most normal in every respect. My daughter was not the only lady on board, as Mrs B. Docker wife of the Chief Engineer, was also on board. I had the loyal co-operation of officers, engineers and crew, and the ladies entered into the venture with zest. I trust this will be the means of other food ships entering the port as I consider there are no risks and cargoes are badly needed.

Roberts, Master – *Seven Seas Spray*

A proud man who was to be held in very high esteem by the Basques. However, no mention of his attempt to try to persuade his daughter to stay at the French port. Nineteen year old Florence Roberts had in fact written to a friend at home telling of her intention to sail with the ship to Bilbao.

… but I am going nevertheless. I am a member of the ship's crew, and although Dad wants me to stay here (St. Jean de Luz) I shall be with the ship when she gets to Bilbao. Make no mistake about that.

How could Captain Roberts have his own way when he had such a determined young daughter.

By coincidence the ship was actually adopted (through the Ship Adoption Society) by Penarth County School for Girls, which Florence Roberts had previously attended. She had written to her former headmistress Miss K. Hughes of her voyage on the ship, giving details of the transfer of ownership of the vessel during the passage, and the details of the cargo which was consigned for delivery at Bilbao. As a result the progress and exploits of the ship were followed by students with great interest and pride.

The arrival of the ship at Bilbao, whilst being welcomed by the hungry people of the city, came as a complete shock to the British Government, The Royal Navy and to General Franco and his Nationalist Navy. The British Government had to admit its mistake in indicating that the port was mined and unsafe, and now gave assurances of protection to ships whilst outside Spanish territorial waters, and instructed the Royal Navy accordingly. The Nationalists were so infuriated by the successful run of the *Seven Seas Spray* that they intensified their blockade of the port, and stated their intention of ensuring that no other ship should make it to Bilbao. The whole world waited with baited breath to see what further developments would take place. Would others follow the *Seven Seas Spray*?

On the day after the successful run into Bilbao by the *Seven Seas Spray*, the Guardian Line's *Macgregor* arrived back at St. Jean de Luz from Bayonne with Captain Owen 'Corn Cob' Jones more determined than ever to make the run. The *Hamsterley* (Captain Still) was still in the port and had already been joined by the steamer *Stanbrook* (Captain Prance). This latter ship was also loaded with foodstuffs (1,840 tons of grain) and was owned by the Stanhope Steamship Co. Ltd., of London and managed by the soon to be legendary figure of the Spanish Civil War, Jack Albert Billmeir.

On arrival at St. Jean de Luz Captain Jones went on board the cruiser HMS *Hood* which was in port and consulted Vice-Admiral Blake about his intentions. As a result of their discussions it was unofficially agreed that HMS *Hood* would be cruising off Bilbao on April 23, which would be the morning after the *Macgregor* and the other two ships would be leaving St. Jean de Luz.

On the evening of April 22 the three ships, *Macgregor, Hamsterley* and *Stanbrook* left St. Jean de Luz in convoy with their precious cargoes. Nationalist Agents were much more alert by now, and news of their departure was quickly passed to the Nationalist Naval forces, who were determined to stop them at all costs. Unlike the *Seven Seas Spray* these ships had absolutely no chance of taking Franco's forces by surprise. They knew the ships were coming, and realistically the masters of the merchantmen knew they knew. The three British ships expected trouble, and they were not to be disappointed, or at least 'Corn Cob' Jones of the *Macgregor*, the leading vessel, wasn't but even he couldn't have forecasted the events which followed.

On the morning of April 23, the ships were by now well spread out. The Nationalist cruiser *Almirante Cervera* accompanied by the armed trawler *Galerna* were patrolling off the coast waiting for them. Fortunately, and to no ones surprise HMS *Hood* and HMS *Firedrake* were also in attendance. When ten miles off Bilbao the Welsh owned *Magregor* was fired on by the *Almirante Cervera*, which put a shell across the merchant ships bow. The British cruiser already prepared for action warned the Spanish cruiser not to interfere with British Shipping, and that if she did not cease firing at the *Macgregor* she would be fired upon herself. The *Hood* and *Firedrake* had their guns trained on the insurgent vessels, and fortunately the *Almirante Cervera* stopped firing. At that stage HMS *Hood* told the *Macgregor* to proceed if she so wished. The Nationalists did not give up their attempt to stop the *Macgregor* however. As the Welsh ship was approaching the three mile limit the armed trawler *Galerna* fired another shell across her bow. HMS *Firedrake* quickly intervened and warned the *Galerna* not to interfere with a British ship in international waters. Before any reaction could be forthcoming the Basque shore battery at Bilbao opened fire at the insurgent vessel, which quickly withdrew from range and the Welsh ship which had been fired on twice proceeded towards the port of Bilbao with the *Hamsterley* and *Stanbrook* close behind, now under the protection of the shore batteries. They entered the port in triumph.

These three cargoes were urgently needed by the Basque people, and again their arrival was watched and cheered by grateful people. Amazingly Captain Prance radioed his owners with 'Arrived 9.30am. Commencing to discharge immediately. Passage from St. Jean de Luz uneventful. No sign of mines or Franco. Everything in order and normal'. If his arrival was normal the ships must have been well spaced out, or were his eyes closed?

Meanwhile other ships were making their way towards Northern Spain. The steamer *Thorpehall* had arrived at La Pallice on April 21 with a cargo of coal loaded at Gijon which she intended to take to Bilbao.

Thereafter the following British ships ran the blockade to arrive in ports in Northern Spain. On April 25 the

The steamer *"Macgregor"* which entered Bilbao on April, 23, 1937.

*(Laurence Dunn)*

Captain Owen "Corn Cob" Jones master of the *"Macgregor"*. *(Western Mail)*

Charles Alan Roberts manager of The Guardian Line of Cardiff, which owned the *"Macgregor"*.

J.A. Billmeir's *"Stanbrook"* entered Bilbao on April 23, 1937.    *(York Collection)*

Newcastle ship *Stesso* docked with a cargo of foodstuffs accompanied by the West Hartlepool ship *Thurston* also with foodstuffs, both having made the run from the French Bay of Biscay port of La Pallice. On the same day the London vessel *Jenny* with foodstuffs from Antwerp, and the Glasgow registered *Oakgrove* with coal from Sunderland made it into Santander. However, the *Oakgrove* was fired on outside territorial waters by a Nationalist warship, and only made port with the intervention of a unit of the Royal Navy. On the following day the *Sheaf Garth* owned by Souter's of Newcastle also made it into Bilbao with a valuable cargo.

On Monday, April 26, 1937 an event was to occur in Northern Spain which was to shock and outrage most of the civilised world. A few miles from the sea lies the small town of Guernica which had a population of about 7,000. This small town, of little military importance to the conflict, was in fact the ancient capital of the Basque Nation. On that

On April 25 the Newcastle steamer *Stesso* made it into Bilbao with a cargo of foodstuffs
*(Laurence Dunn collection)*

48

The steamer *Oakgrove* of Glasgow made it into Santander on April 25, following intervention by the Royal Navy.

*(John Clarkson)*

date commencing at 4.40pm the German Condor Legions attacked the town and systematically destroyed it in waves of attacks with Heinkel 111 and Junkers 52 aircraft; bombing and machine-gunning the civilian population mercilessly. The centre of the town was destroyed by the end of the attack at 7.45pm, leaving 1,654 people dead and 889 wounded. This single act represented the greatest sin of the war to the Spanish people; it was also the first case in history of the saturation bombing of a defenceless civilian population. Clearly the German and Italian forces were gaining much experience in Spain, and regarded it as a proving ground for their troops and equipment. The world was outraged. General Franco was severely embarrassed, and it was to take over thirty years in Spain before people were publically able to refer to it without fear of prosecution.

The people of Bilbao did not go unscathed either. All through this period Bilbao was suffering heavy air attacks, and indeed General Franco had warned British shipping that they would be specifically sought out as targets. As a result on that day the steamer *Hamsterley,* which had arrived on April 23 was hit and damaged. Fortunately no one was hurt and the damage was not sufficient to stop her leaving the port when she had completed her business.

At midnight on April 19, actually a matter of hours after the *Seven Seas Spray* had sailed from St. Jean de Luz on her legendary voyage to Bilbao, the Non-Intervention Committee's Naval patrol came into effect. This assigned the Mediterranean part of the Republic coast to Italy and Germany (which seems like a mistake), the Basque/Santander coast to Britain, and the Nationalist held coast to both France and Britain. There was no patrol of the Portuguese coastline, although a few British observers were allowed on Portugal's frontier with Spain and observers were stationed on the French/Spanish border. Non-Intervention Committee control officers were also carried from that date on ships going to and from Spain, thus ensuring as far as possible that arms were not carried.

Very early in the conflict the British Government had banned the export of arms to either side, although, initially this did not prohibit British flag ships from carrying arms, as long as it was from some other country. Later in 1936 they made specific legislation, in the form of the Merchant Shipping (Carriage of Munitions to Spain) Act, 1936, to prohibit entirely the carriage of armaments in British ships. Only one British master mariner was ever charged with the offence, and as will be shown later, even he was acquitted. Although a number of British ships were actually suspected by the Royal Navy of carrying arms to Spain, and a careful watch was kept, and examinations made of suspected vessels and cargoes, none was found.

Prior to the breaking of the blockade of Bilbao by the *Seven Seas Spray* on the morning of April 20, the plight of the Basque people was the subject of great concern to many individuals and organisations in Britain. The Trade Union movement were particularly concerned with the well being of the starving people of Bilbao, as was the International League of Friends, and the church. Lloyd George had even publically declared himself to be a 'Basque'. These organisations and people combined their resources and set about attempting to charter a ship to send to Bilbao. Offers of food were accepted and other supplies purchased with donations, and after some difficulty in finding a shipowner prepared to allow his vessel to be used, they succeeded in chartering the steamer *Backworth* owned by the Dalgliesh

Steam Shipping Co. Ltd., of Newcastle. The ship was loaded at Immingham, and prepared for the voyage. Many people wanted to sail on her, but the owners of the ship insisted that the only people who were to go were those who were needed to sail the ship, ie the crew, with the mandatory Non-Intervention Committee Control Officer. At last, on April 23 the *Backworth* set out from Immingham under the command of Captain Russell, on her mission of mercy. She carried a much needed cargo of Foodstuffs together with medical supplies and the like.

On April 28, five days after sailing from the United Kingdom, she arrived off the North Spanish coast, and by arrangement was met by the battleship HMS *Royal Oak* and the destroyer HMS *Fury*, at this time the Nationalist warship *Espana* was operating in the vicinity, and at the same time as the *Backworth* arrived declaring her intention to enter Bilbao, the Consett Iron Company's steamer *Consett* arrived off Santander declaring her intention to make that port. The *Espana* actually covered Santander and as a result the *Royal Oak* left the *Backworth* in the charge of the *Fury* and made off to assess the situation further West. Seeing what the situation off Santander was, and that the *Espana* was in attendance the *Royal Oak* warned the master of the *Consett* against trying to make Santander, and in fact the merchant ship altered course to seaward and the following day arrived at St. Jean de Luz.

Meanwhile the *Fury* advised the *Backworth* from trying to enter Bilbao, but Captain Russell, declared his determination to proceed with his cargo to that port at all costs. The destroyer accompanied the vessel towards the three mile limit and then the *Backworth* steamed at full speed toward Bilbao, where she arrived without having been molested by Nationalist Naval forces. Captain Russell on his arrival sent the following radio message to the press in London via Bordeaux Port Radio, although in parts it was jammed by the Nationalists.

> We nipped in two days ahead in rain swept ocean. Sighted *Fury*, four thirty alongside and megaphoned "You will be bombed or fired on if caught do you intend to proceed Captain Russell". – "We intend to Proceed". Cheers from *Fury* and our crew started (blocked) running three miles (blocked) *Fury* had cleared decks for action. Our enterprise in best tradition of Captain Blood – *Backworth* had never travelled so fast belching black smoke over bay, took Pilot aboard seven now entering harbour, behaviour of crew magnificent, our lifeboats were all ready expecting fire from Spaniard any minute.

On this occasion the merchant ship was actually assisted by the diversion which was set up by the *Consett* trying to make Santander. The *Backworth* was now the eighth ship to have entered Bilbao since the blockade was broken eight

The *"Backworth"* entered Bilbao on April 28, 1937. She had been chartered as a result of public subscription to carry foodstuffs. She is shown under her later name of *"Ogmore Castle"*.

(E.N. Taylor)

days earlier. The Basques realised that this ship's cargo was rather special as it had been provided by public subscription to help them in their hour of need, and was much appreciated.

The following day four more cargoes were delivered in Bilbao by British ships. At 8am on April 29 the steamers *Marvia* of London, *Thorpehall* of London, *Sheaf Field* of Newcastle and *Portelet* of Guernsey arrived outside territorial waters where by arrangement HMS *Royal Oak* met them. There was no attempt by the Nationalists to prevent their entry, and all four ships made Bilbao without incident. However, not long after their arrival they were attacked by fifteen bombers, which were described by observers as German, which fortunately were unable to score a hit, although damage in the port area was extensive.

A day later the steamer *Consett* again turned up off Santander in an effort to enter port, but again had to turn to seaward as she was shelled by the *Espana*, which fortunately did not hit her and failed to capture her.

Later that day the British steamer *Knitsley* which was also owned by the Consett Iron Company attempted to make the small port of Castro Urdiales, which is between Bilbao and Santander. On her approach to the coast she was ordered to stop by the Nationalist destroyer *Velasco* which fired a shot, whilst in the distance the battleship *Espana* could be seen. The *Knitsley* had not complied with this order when she heard an explosion from the direction of the *Espana* and then saw a number of Republican aircraft attacking the Nationalist vessel. The reports which were made of this incident were confusing, but whatever, the *Knitsley* saw the battleship sinking, the *Velasco* gave up her attempt to stop the merchant ship to go to the assistance of her countrymen. The *Knitsley* didn't waste any time, and slipped into the port where she took on a much needed cargo of iron ore. Whilst the Republican aircraft had indeed gone to the aid of the *Knitsley* it is apparent that the *Espana* was actually sunk by a mine which she had struck. The loss of this warship by the Nationalists gave the Basque people a much needed boost to their moral.

On this same day the fishing port of Bermeo, near Bilbao, was captured by a contingent of Italian troops, but as the war in the North progressed these soldiers were surrounded and had to beg relief.

Thereafter British merchant ships managed to enter and leave Bilbao with their important cargoes, and were little interfered with. However, the Nationalists increased the effectiveness of the blockade of Santander and Gijon, and as such merchant ships tended to wait in numbers off these ports, and outside territorial waters for the ideal moment to run the blockade. Some were fired on, and as will be seen in a later chapter a number captured. As regards Bilbao a number of British ships were to enter and leave the port, including Alfred Pope's *Joyce Llewellyn*, (later renamed *Seabank)*, and *Kenfig Pool*, Claude Angel's *Bramhill*, *Hillfern* and *Yorkbrook*, and the *Candleston Castle* owned by Reginald Jones of Cardiff.

On May 5 the *Hamsterley* was pursued by an insurgent warship as she made her way out of Bilbao to the open sea. Although fired on she succeeded in reaching international waters, and the protection of the *Royal Oak*. It was now becoming apparent that Bilbao was likely to fall to the Nationalists, and as a result many Basque people wanted to leave Spain and escape the consequences of being at the mercy of General Franco's troops. This was reflected in the departure of the *Hamsterley*, as she carried a number of such refugees to safety.

On the evening of that same day and throughout that night 4,000 women and children embarked on the Basque liner *Habana* and motor yacht *Goizeko Izarra* at Bilbao intending to flee to the safety of France. Many were ultimately destined to go on to the United Kingdom where there was considerable support for their cause. However, these two ships left the port on the morning of May 6 flying the Basque flag and that of the International Red Cross. Orders had been given to the Royal Navy by the British Government to protect these vessels from the insurgent threat when, and only when, they reached international waters. As a result they steamed at full speed to depart from the three mile limit as fast as possible, where the battleship *Royal Oak* was waiting. Also in attendance and waiting to shell and sink them was the Nationalist cruiser *Almirante Cervera*. These ships, being Spanish could lawfully be interfered with by the Nationalist vessel outside the three mile limit, and the commander of the insurgent vessel plainly conveyed his intentions to the *Royal Oak*, "I have orders to sink the convoy". To which the *Royal Oak* replied "We have orders to protect the convoy outside the three mile limit". When the refugee ships reached the three mile limit, the Royal Navy set out to protect them by stationing destroyers and the *Royal Oak* around them so that any ship firing at them would also be firing at the British warships. It was an excellent tactic as the Nationalists could not risk this and departed from the scene. These Basque vessels made numerous voyages from Bilbao and later Santander evacuating women and children to French ports, and the *Habana* even took one group of 4,000 to Southampton.

Food shortages in Bilbao were still very apparent. Any British ship delayed in the port also suffered from this problem, and as a result British seamen usually shared out their provisions in these circumstances. A ship leaving port would take with her only sufficient for the passage and leave the balance for their countrymen.

The Spanish tanker *Campero* was torpedoed by a submarine between the ports of Palamos and San Feliu de Guixoles while bound for Barcelona. There were no casualties, and the vessel which was in ballast did not sink. She managed with difficulty to make it into Palamos, but she was severely damaged.

The Spanish vessel *Rapido* was set on fire and sunk by an unknown submarine. The six man crew of the vessel spent a night at sea before arriving at Alicante in a small boat. They had been stopped by the submarine and told to abandon her. When they were in the boat the submarine opened fire with a small gun and set the *Rapido* on fire fore and aft and they saw the vessel sink rapidly.

The Danish steamer *Dorrit* was taken for a second time in the Straits and released at Ceuta after a short delay. Her cargo was complete. Another vessel taken into Ceuta for a second visit was the Russian *Transbalt,* but again the vessel was later released. The steamer *Start* was also so treated. Another Russian stopped and later freed was the *Kuban.*

## Chapter 6

# THE BLOCKADE OF NORTHERN SPAIN AFTER THE FALL OF BILBAO

Although historians refer to the blockade of Northern Spain from April to October 1937 collectively as the Blockade of Bilbao, I have for convenience split the period into two chapters; that up to the fall of Bilbao in an earlier chapter, and that after in this.

As a result of the fall of Bilbao, the Basque Government chartered a considerable number of ships to carry refugees from Northern Spain. The ports still in Republican hands, such as Santander, Musel, Santona and Gijon, were crowded with refugees who were trying to flee from the Nationalist advance. The influx of people into these areas caused great strain on the already low food stocks, and the ships entering to embark these refugees in some cases brought food supplies with them. Some ships were actually employed running back and forth between Northern Spain and France only carrying personnel.

A considerable number of these ships were owned or managed in South Wales, but as will be seen other British flag vessels were also involved. On June 22 the Hong Kong ship *Marion Moller* was stopped outside territorial waters by the Nationalist armed vessel *Ciudad de Palma*. At this time the *Marion Moller* had just left Santander with as many women and children as she could carry, and immediately sent out a distress call to the Royal Navy. The call was answered by the destroyer HMS *Boadicea* which was sent to her assistance, and on arrival warned the Nationalist vessel, which then left the scene. The British merchant ship was then escorted to St. Jean de Luz where the French authorities refused to allow the refugees to land. Thereafter she was ordered to proceed to Pauillac, near Bordeaux where arrangements were made to handle her human cargo of over 2,000 souls.

On June 30 the Newport steamer *Gwenthills* was approaching the Spanish Coast intending to enter Castro Urdiales to pick up a cargo of iron ore, when she was warned by HMS *Boreas* that the port was now in insurgent hands. She then decided to make for St. Jean de Luz to await orders, but a short while later was fired on by an armed insurgent trawler outside territorial waters. She did not stop and continued for the French port where she arrived the following day. This ship was owned by Mordey, Son and Co. Ltd., of 46, Commercial Street, Newport, Monmouthshire, whose steamer *Gwentland* was sold in 1937 to become Claude Angel's *Bramhill*. The *Gwenthills* (868 gross tons) was a newbuilding of smaller dimensions.

During July 1937 the Royal Navy were hard pressed to supervise the vast number of British ships which started to lie off Northern Spanish ports awaiting the opportunity to run in to embark refugees. All were steaming outside the three mile limit and also presented a major problem to the Nationalist Navy, who had difficulty in covering all the ports. The British merchantmen knew this and were prepared to wait their best chance of evading capture before proceeding into territorial waters.

On July 4 the French steamer *Tregastel* misjudged her opportunity and was captured by the cruiser *Almirante Cervera*. Four shells were fired across her bows before the steamer submitted and was escorted to the now Nationalist held Bilbao. The following day, our old friend the *Seven Seas Spray* turned up off Santander with a cargo from Valencia. She was advised by the Royal Navy not to try to enter the port and as a result her master, Captain W.H. Roberts made for Bayonne where he communicated with the owner, Alfred Pope, and thereafter awaited orders. The following day the British ship *Gordonia* found it impossible to get past the Nationalist blockade off Santander and made for Bordeaux to await orders. She had actually been stopped by the torpedo boat *No. 7* and the cruiser *Almirante Cervera* before the destroyers HMS *Escapade* and HMS *Bulldog* intervened to rescue her.

The *Royal Oak* was off Northern Spain from July 11 and observed three Welsh owned ships waiting their chance. These were the *Molton* owned by Lord Glanely, the *Sarastone* of Stone and Rolfe and the *Kenfig Pool* owned by Alfred Pope. The *Kenfig Pool* declared her intention to the British battleship of entering Santander at all costs, but when the Nationalist cruiser *Almirante Cervera* turned up she steamed out to sea again.

Support in Wales for the Basque people was magnificent. A Cardiff Committee of the National Joint Committee for Spanish Relief was established to maintain fifty Basque children at Cambria House, Caerleon, Monmouthshire. The home opened on

Reginald Jones' *"Candleston Castle"* (ex *"Seven Seas Star"*) was captured by General Franco's Forces off Gijon on July 17, 1937.                                                                                                 *(Welsh Industrial & Maritime Museum)*

complement of refugees, and successfully made it out into international waters. There was an uproar in the press in Britain, where it was not understood, or they did not want to understand how and why a British man-of-war was powerless to protect a British merchantman whilst in the territorial waters of another Sovereign State. On July 19 Anthony Eden, the Foreign Secretary made the following statement regarding the *Molton,* in the House of Commons:

> I understand that the steamer *Molton* was chartered on July 1 by the Basque Government agent in
> London for the purpose of evacuating civilian refugees from Northern Spain to French ports.
> Instructions have been sent to H.M. Ambassador at Hendaye to demand the release of the vessel and
> of her crew and to state that His Majesty's Government must hold General Franco's Government
> responsible for any injury or damage she may have incurred. It is reported in the Press that the ship
> is about to be released. I have not been able to confirm that.

On the afternoon after the capture of the *Molton* the Welsh steamer *Kellwyn* turned up off Santander hoping to enter. This ship was none other than the *Marie Llewellyn* under a new guise, but still commanded by the colourful character 'Potato' Jones. On being warned by HMS *Royal Oak* of the morning's activities she steamed off to the West and entered Gijon which was not so heavily blockaded. This ship brought out 800 refugees.

On July 15 the *Kenfig Pool* put back into Bayonne for bunkers and fresh water, before making further efforts to enter Santander. On that same day two attempts were made by the London registered *Thorpebay* to enter Santander, but on each occasion she was warned against doing so by the two British destroyers lying off the port. The Santander authorities claimed that on both occasions the channel was clear and that no insurgent vessel was in sight.

In the evening of July 15 the Cardiff owned *Nailsea Vale* attempted to enter Santander to take off refugees, but in response to signals from a British destroyer she altered course and steamed away. At the time the cruiser *Almirante Cervera* was in the offing. The merchant ship had previously carried a number of refugees out of this port, and was eventually to succeed again.

The *Sarastone* and Reginald Jones's *Candleston Castle* which had originally intended to enter Santander to board women and children, changed their minds and on July 17 headed for Gijon. Both had been off the coast for some days, and decided their chances would be better further to the West. However, as they neared the port of Musel near Gijon and inside territorial waters they were fired on by the Nationalist warships *Valesco* and *Plus Ultra*. Unfortunately the *Candleston Castle* was captured and taken into the Nationalist port of Ferrol, whilst the *Sarastone* managed to reach Gijon by sailing close into the coast where she was protected by coastal batteries.

Subsequently Reginald Jones received the following cable from his ship:

Anchored Ferrol Harbour yesterday, July 18, remaining here pending inquiry, please advise relatives all well on board. British Consul Corunna arrived and rendering us all assistance.

The owner of this ship, Reginald Jones was a shrewd character who was renowned for seizing opportunities when they presented themselves who traded as Reginald Jones and Co. Ltd., with offices at first at Merthyr House, James Street, Cardiff, but later at Empire House, 51, Mount Stuart Square, Cardiff. He had previously been a partner in McNeil and Jones since 1915 but formed his own company in 1933 to manage the Branch Steamship Co. Ltd., which he had established in that same year. He never operated a big fleet, and indeed only owned a single ship most of the time. He had taken delivery of the *Candlestone Castle* which had previously been Walter Vaughan's *Seven Seas Star* at Bordeaux in March, 1937. Reggie Jones lived at the Brig-y-Don Hotel, Ogmore, Glamorgan, which he owned. Thus he had lost the use of his only ship for a while.

On July 19 the steamer *Jenny* succeeded in entering Gijon, while the *Thorpebay* joined the *Marvia* waiting off Santander.

Also in July Lord Glanely's steamer *Pilton* carried many refugees out of Santander, and on July 27 dashed into Aviles and subsequently carried another batch of refugees out to France.

On July 22 the *Macgregor* under the command of Captain Owen 'Corn Cob' Jones was to have another run in with the Nationalist cruiser *Almirante Cervera* off Northern Spain. On that date the *Macgregor* left Santander with over 2,000 refugees on board destined for the French port of Pauillac. On leaving she was signalled to by the *Almirante Cervera* inside the three mile limit, to stop. Captain Jones took no notice, and the cruiser then fired two warning shots across the Welsh Merchantman's bows. Again Captain Jones ignored the order from the Nationalist to stop, whereupon two more shells were fired across her bows. 'Corn Cob' Jones never faltered for a minute and steamed at full speed for international waters, knowing full well what fate was likely to befall his cargo of unfortunate Basques if he were to submit to the insurgent warship. All on board were plainly relieved when the *Macgregor* cleared territorial waters and came immediately under the protection of HMS *Kempenfelt* which was waiting off the port and had witnessed events with great concern. As a result of this the captain of the *Almirante Cervera* immediately represented to the British Naval Authorities that the *Macgregor* in not obeying the order to stop had taken advantage of his humanitarian feelings, but that she would not take any further action. It is true that the cruiser could have sunk the *Macgregor* if she had wanted, but Captain Jones did not care a hoot, he had done what he was paid to do, and fulfilled his obligation to the now exiled Basque Government.

Two days later, on July 24 the *Backworth* also left Santander with a couple of thousand refugees also destined for France.

On that same day the Welsh managed steamer *African Trader* entered territorial waters off Gijon fully intending to make that port to embark more refugees, however she was ordered to stop by the insurgent cruiser *Baleares*. The British ship ignored this instruction, and what looked like a dangerous incident was rapidly getting out of control. Seeing the situation from outside the three mile limit HMS *Escapade* went up as far to the ship as she was allowed and signalled for her to come out of territorial waters. The *African Trader* complied with this and thereafter came under the protection of HMS *Escapade* and HMS *Royal Oak*. The latter vessel sent a boarding party to the merchantman to check that she was bona fides, and then escorted her back to the safety of St. Jean de Luz. However, the British merchant ship was not finished, and she did eventually make it to Gijon.

Later that day the British steamer *Mirupanu* which was also making for Gijon was captured off the port inside the three mile limit by the insurgent ship *Ciudad de Valencia,* and thereafter escorted to Ferrol for examination and enquiry.

Referring to the *African Trader* she was managed by David P. Barnett from Baltic House, Mount Stuart Square, Cardiff. He had been involved in shipowning and management since 1916 and by 1936 was managing a single ship, the *Penthames* on behalf of the Golden Cross Line (Bristol Channel) Ltd. However during the period of the Civil War he became responsible for managing a fleet of truly gigantic size which was all registered at London in the ownership of the following companies – The African & Continental Steamship Co. Ltd. (later restyled as the African and Continental Steamship and Trading Co. Ltd.), the Atlantic & Mediterranean Trading Co. Ltd., and the Continental Transit Co. Ltd., as follows:–

| Name | Year built | Year acquired | Gross tons | Remarks |
|------|-----------|---------------|-----------|---------|
| *Penthames* | 1909 | 1936 | 1,988 | Sold in 1937 |
| *Penthames* | 1913 | 1937 | 3,995 | |

| | | | |
|---|---|---|---|
| *African Mariner* | 1920 | 1937 | 6,581 |
| *Sunion* | 1919 | 1937 | 3,110 |
| *African Explorer* | 1919 | 1938 | 4,663 |
| *African Trader* | 1908 | 1937 | 3,825 |
| *Lulca* | 1907 | 1938 | 4,657 |
| *Cemenco* | 1927 | 1938 | 1,887 |
| *Emerald Wings* | 1920 | 1938 | 2,139 |
| *Trade* | 1912 | 1938 | 5,848 |
| *Transeas* | 1924 | 1938 | 1,499 |
| *Transit* | 1919 | 1938 | 3,091 |
| *Atlantic Scout* | 1912 | 1938 | 4,575 |
| *Burrington Combe* | 1910 | 1939 | 4,000 |
| *Atlantic Guide* | 1924 | 1939 | 1,943 |

On July 27 the Hong Kong registered steamer *Marion Moller* was turned back off Santander. She had been chartered by the National Joint Committee for Spanish Relief and was carrying £500 worth of food and £700 worth of medical supplies. The medical supplies consisted of a quantity of anti-gas gangrene serum, specially requested by the Republican authorities, anaesthetics, and anti-typhoid Serum. Again, the following day she was blockaded off Gijon. But eventually she made it into a Northern port with her much needed cargo.

On July 27 the steamers *Sarastone* and *Tuskar Rock* were able to leave Gijon with thousands of refugees without interference by the insurgent navy. On July 29 there were actually three ships blockaded off Santander awaiting an opportunity to make a dash for port, these were the steamer *Marvia*, the British ship *Bobie* which was owned by a relative of Thomas McEwen, and was actually registered at Gibraltar, and the tanker *Valetta* owned by Jas. German and Co. Ltd., Cardiff., and which was subsequently renamed *Arlon*. All three eventually broke the blockade, but which ports they managed to enter, I do not know, other than the *Bobie* which made Santona, near Santander.

Such was the concern of the Admiralty concerning the situation off Northern Spain, that they felt it necessary to actually define Spanish territorial waters. As a result the Board of Trade made the following announcement to British shipowners, on July 30.

> Owners and masters of British vessels should note that, as a working arrangement for the purposes of the present emergency only, territorial water off Santander and Gijon are to be regarded as extending to the three miles from:
> (a)    In the case of Santander, a line from Cape Ajo to Cape Lata.
> (b)    In the case of Gijon, a line from Cape de Torres to Cape San Lorenzo.

These arrangements extended the three mile limit somewhat, but it made it easier for merchantmen and the Royal Navy alike to know their respective positions exactly.

Although Bilbao had fallen as early as June 19, the British Government had prior to that date, even with this situation existing between British merchantmen and the insurgent Navy, been involved in secret negotiations with General Franco to ensure that when the port fell they would still secure continuity of supplies from the iron ore mines. Resulting from the negotiations General Franco agreed to allow sixty per cent of the iron ore production to be exported to Britain. The Italians and Germans were very angry about this agreement. When Hitler and Mussolini had come to Franco's aid, Germany had been allowed a substantial part of the minerals being exported through Huelva, and had expected similar treatment regarding the Northern deposits, particularly in view of the support being given to the Nationalist cause.

Whilst British ships were involved in confrontation with Nationalist forces off Northern Spain between Santander and Gijon, other shipowners resumed trading to Bilbao to load iron ore quite happily, and almost oblivious to the events being enacted a little way off to the West. Constants (South Wales) Ltd resumed carrying supplies on behalf of G.K.N. and other owners quickly followed. Franco, would not, however, allow any ship to enter Bilbao, if it had previously traded with Republican held ports during the conflict.

On August 3 the Board of Trade made the following announcement regarding the situation at Bilbao.

> The following information in regard to the conditions of shipping at Bilbao, based upon information obtained from the Naval Authorities in control of that port, has been reported by His Majesty's Ambassador at Hendaye: There are no mines or other obstructions in the channels leading to the port of Bilbao, but pilotage is compulsory for all vessels. British vessels are required to give 72

hours' notice of their arrival in order to enable berthing to be allotted and due notice should be sent to the Naval Authority at Bilbao or to Captain Caveda, the Officer-in-Command of the region. The Naval Commandant at Bilbao will allot the berth and vessels must conform exactly with his order. The local Spanish Naval Authorities state that merchant vessels which have been trading with ports under the control of the Spanish Government will not be allowed to use the port, except that in case of *force majeure* they may enter the port, though they will not be allowed to remain more than 24 hours.

This announcement meant in effect that if a shipowner had used one of his ships in the Republican or Basque cause, that ship would be prevented from docking, but if he owned another ship which had not gone to such ports that ship would not be disallowed.

Returning to the situation further to the West, on August 11 the British steamer *Caper* was captured by the Nationalist vessel *Tritonia* off Cape Vidio and taken under escort to Rivadeo for examination and enquiry.

On August 12, in view of the tens of thousands of Spanish refugees which had been entering France on British ships, the French Government announced that in future:

No Spanish refugees will be allowed to land in France, unless disembarkation in France has been authorised by the French Government in each individual case.

They specifically requested the British Government to inform immediately the masters of British vessels concerned with the carriage of refugees from Spain. France, being sympathetic to the Republicans, had done more than most, but they were now declaring that they could not take any more. However, they did in fact take more, and many were resettled outside France. Britain had always made it known that no ship would be allowed to bring refugees to the United Kingdom, but they played their part by taking some of those which had transitted via France. The announcement was ignored by British shipowners right up until the fall of the last ports in October 1937.

On August 16, two Welsh ships left Northern ports with refugees, totalling 5,600 in number, with complete disregard for the French announcement. The Cardiff steamer *Nailsea Vale* from Aviles and the Newport registered *Bramhill* from Gijon. Neither was intercepted by insurgent forces, and all their unfortunate passengers were subsequently disembarked in France.

On August 25 Santander and Santona fell. The insurgent forces actually taking Santander whilst Santona was taken by Italian troops. Alfred Pope's ships figured heavily at this time as the *Seabank* and *Kenfig Pool* were at Santander while the *Seven Seas Spray* and the chartered *Bobie* were at Santona. All four had been chartered by the Basque Government to carry refugees to France, but had been caught in port before they could embark due to the confusion existing. Because Santona was taken by Italian troops the Basque representatives there actually managed to negotiate to evacuate thousands of their countrymen on the ships. Permission was granted on August 27 to the master of the *Bobie*, a Frenchman, Georges Dupuy, and a Non-Intervention Observer on the *Seven Seas Spray*, Costa e Silva, a Brazilian, for the embarkation to take place. However, General Franco was soon to intervene to stop the ships leaving, and the following day all were taken off and marched down the quay, some for imprisonment and many for eventual execution. Thereafter the *Bobie* was allowed to leave, and she quickly set off for France with seven stowaways on board. However, Captain W.H. Roberts was not allowed to follow with the *Seven Seas Spray*, probably being the price of breaking the blockade of Bilbao in April, and the ship and crew were detained in the port. Alfred Pope was luckier with the *Seabank* and *Kenfig Pool* as they were allowed to leave Santander on September 2 and made for a French port.

Numerous air attacks were now concentrated on Gijon, and on August 27 the four ships in the port were damaged by bombs. These were the Welsh managed *African Trader* which started taking in water forward as a result of the damage, the Jack Billmeir ships *Stanwood* and *Stanbridge,* and the Moller Line's *Hilda Moller*. The masters of these ships now considered that the ports of Northern Spain were too dangerous and the *African Trader, Stanwood* and *Hilda Moller* sailed from the port without delay. The *Stanbridge* was unable to weigh anchor due to the damage, but managed to leave on September 11. The worst damaged ship was the *African Trader* commanded by Captain Bullock. Such was the concern that HMS *Fearless* and HMS *Foresight* were sent to accompany her in case she should founder on route to La Pallice. The damage was so bad, that her pumps were only just able to keep her afloat, and on arrival at the French port she had to be beached immediately to prevent her from sinking. She was subsequently refloated, drydocked, and following repairs sailed about a month later for Cardiff.

Having safely left Gijon on August 16, the *Bramhill* re-entered the war zone on route from Brest back to Gijon, when on August 28 at 6pm she was sighted by two insurgent trawlers near the port. The insurgents considered that the Welsh ship was inside territorial waters and fired a warning shot to order her to stop. The master of the *Bramhill* did not

After two months detention and repeated representations from the British Government on September 10 the Nationalists released the steamer *Molton*.

consider he was within territorial waters and refused to stop, as a result a further shot was fired across her bows. Again she refused to comply. At that stage HMS *Fearless* arrived to investigate and after an exchange of signals, it was confirmed that the *Bramhill* was still outside the three mile limit, and she was allowed to proceed (to seaward) and the incident was closed.

Following the success of his land forces General Franco was able to tighten his blockade of Gijon and Aviles as the Nationalist fleet under the cruiser *Almirante Cervera* had a much shorter length of coastline to patrol. As a result, even the ever persistent *Thorpehall* returned to Bayonne on September 7 having been prevented from entering Gijon.

At 10pm on September 8 the Billmeir steamer *Stanwold* was captured by an insurgent vessel within territorial waters off Rivadesella, within sight of HMS *Resolution*. The *Stanwold* had been observed outside the three mile limit by the British warship, which had warned her that she was approaching territorial waters. Almost immediately after she crossed the three mile limit an insurgent torpedo boat which had been hovering on the horizon, gathered speed, overtook the *Stanwold* and fired three warning shots. The *Stanwold* altered course and proceeded accompanied by the torpedo boat, in the direction of an insurgent port. When HMS *Resolution* asked if he had anything to report, the master of the *Stanwold* wirelessed "I am captured".

However, the Royal Navy were not exactly happy with this turn of events, and it was certainly their belief that the merchant ship, having been paid to carry the cargo in advance had actually allowed herself to be captured, by arrangement as it were, in order to sell the cargo to the Nationalist forces. I leave the reader to judge for himself.

After repeated representations from the British Government, on September 10 the Welsh steamers, *Molton* owned by Lord Glanely and which had been captured on July 14, and the *Candleston Castle* which had been taken by Nationalist forces on July 17 and which was owned by Reginald Jones, were released, and allowed to leave Spanish waters. Both ships made for Bordeaux, where they communicated with their respective owners.

On that same day the Claude Angel steamer *Hillfern* which was making for Gijon, was attacked by an insurgent armed trawler when about 35 miles off the coast. Although shelled she was not hit, and she immediately turned away from the Spanish coast. Shortly after she was machine-gunned by aircraft, which appeared to be trying to hit her deck cargo of drums of oil. The ship was undamaged in the incidents. The *Hillfern* arrived at Bayonne on September 12 to await developments and further instructions from Cardiff.

On September 15 the Billmeir steamer *Stanmore* which had set out from La Pallice for Rivadesella to pick up refugees was attacked by aircraft, which fortunately missed. She continued to sail Westwards along the Spanish coast, but decided to turn back when a shore battery opened fire on her. Undamaged she put back to Bordeaux arriving on September 16.

On October 3 the steamer *Bobie* which was carrying a cargo of foodstuffs from Antwerp for either Aviles or Gijon was intercepted off the coast and taken into Rivadeo, and later taken to Ferrol where she arrived on October 6. This ship had been allowed to leave Santona a month earlier when that port fell to the insurgents. She did not carry any British crew members whatsoever, but was owned by Mr. W.H. McEwen of Parkston, Dorset, who was related to Thomas McEwen the partner of Alfred Pope, the by now famous Welsh shipowner engaged in the Spanish trade. The ship was registered at Gibraltar and was flying the British flag, and was actually chartered in by Alfred Pope who had re-chartered it out to the Republican Government.

On Tuesday, October 5 two British ships were captured off Northern Spain. The London registered *Dover Abbey* was not in territorial waters, but unfortunately was not in sight of British warships who would have acted to rescue her in these circumstances. She was carrying a cargo of maize and dried peas from Antwerp to Gijon, and was manned by a crew of nineteen of which thirteen were British; her master was Captain A.E. Jackson of London.

The insurgents must have had great pleasure in taking the other ship that day, as she was none other than the *Yorkbrook* which they had captured once before and lost. Last time she flew the Estonian flag but now she was flying the British flag and was registered at Swansea under the ownership of Claude Angel. She had been chartered to the Spanish Government to carry refugees from Gijon to Bordeaux, and was trying to enter Gijon at the time of her capture.

As the net closed around Gijon and Aviles the passage of British merchantmen to and from these ports became more dangerous. Not only were they being hampered by the Nationalist Navy but they were now equally as likely to be attacked from the air or shelled by the shore batteries.

On October 20, the day before Gijon fell, the Billmeir ship *Stangrove* with nearly 600 refugees on board was captured just after leaving the port by an armed trawler. However it became clear that the ship had made it to International waters and on the arrival of HMS *Southampton* on the scene she demanded that the merchantman be released. The commander of the cruiser *Almirante Cervera* released the vessel under protest, and thereafter the *Southampton* escorted her from the war zone.

Finally the war in the North came to an end on October 21, 1937 when Gijon, Musel and Aviles were taken by the Nationalists.

Six days after the taking of the last Northern stronghold by General Franco's forces the Billmeir steamer *Stanray* was intercepted by an armed trawler outside the three mile limit off Aviles. What she was doing no one knows, but being outside territorial waters, the Royal Navy responded to her distress call and released her.

With the war in the North over General Franco gradually allowed the British ships captured by his forces, to be released. The *Molton* and *Candleston Castle* had been released a month earlier, and the others followed:–

| Name | Date Released |
| --- | --- |
| *Seven Seas Spray* | 1.11.1937 |
| *Stanwold* | 1.11.1937 |
| *Caper* | 12.11.1937 |
| *Mirupanu* | 13.11.1937 |
| *Bobie* | 13.11.1937 |
| *Dover Abbey* | 15.11.1937 |
| *Yorkbrook* | 20.11.1937 |

The only Briton on the *Caper* had been the master and the *Mirupanu* carried none at all.

During the detention of the *Caper* at Ferrol an incident occurred between the six armed guards put on board the ship and members of the crew, and three were shot dead, a Dutchman and two Russians. The master Captain Cossintine was wounded with a bullet in his chest, and was treated ashore. He later returned to the ship but subsequently handed command over to a relief sent out by the owners.

This manning of British flag ships by foreign nationals was a point that both the Nationalists and Royal Navy were

The *"Stanray"* which had been built in 1904 was acquired by Jack Billmeir in 1937. She was broken up a year later.
*(Welsh Industrial & Maritime Museum)*

acutely aware of. It transpired that foreign owners were transferring their ships to the British flag in order to obtain a measure of protection from the Royal Navy, which no other navy had undertaken to do. The Admiralty were less than pleased to be seen protecting foreign nationals sailing foreign owned ships but flying the British flag. This resulted from temporary certificates of British registry being granted, in many cases by British Consuls abroad. A tightening of the rules was surely called for.

# Chapter 7
# ATTACKS IN THE MEDITERRANEAN

Such had been the situation in the Mediterranean, with ships being attacked by submarines, aircraft and occasionally a surface warship, and the claims and counter claims that Italy was primarily responsible, that on June 23, 1937 both Italy and Germany had withdrawn from the Naval Patrol in the Mediterranean. Portugal soon demanded the withdrawal of British observers from their frontier with Spain, and on July 12 France withdrew the facility from her border, which was in fact closed anyhow. The attacks continued, and the cost to Russia, particularly, was so great that she informed the Republican Government that whilst supplies would continue to be provided that in future Spain would have to arrange the shipping to carry them. This resulted in an even greater participation by British flag vessels, as more and more they were sent to the Black Sea to load for Spain. However, the overall effect was to reduce the supplies reaching the Republic.

Britain and France were so concerned by the attacks in the Mediterranean that on September 6 all states with Mediterranean frontiers together with Germany, but excluding both sides in the Spanish conflict, were invited to attend a conference to be held at Nyon in Switzerland commencing on the 10th. Germany and Italy proposed that the matter should be dealt with by the Non-Intervention Committee, but this was unacceptable to Britain and France. In the end Hitler and Mussolini boycotted the conference, but the result was to see decisions made whereby France and Britain would jointly patrol the Mediterranean, and that any unidentified submarine, warship or aircraft whether inside or outside Spanish Territorial Waters would be liable to be attacked by the British and French forces. Subsequently Italy at her own request asked to join the patrol. This agreement did not solve the problem associated with attacks by the two warring Spanish parties, but this was the risk that merchant shipowners had to reconcile themselves with, and few withdrew from the trade because of it.

Meanwhile the war in the South continued. On June 17, 1937 the Italian steamer *Madda* on a voyage to Glasgow was bombed by two Spanish Republican aircraft off Oran, and although no direct hit was recorded concussion damage flooded the forepeak and No. 1 hold. The ship put into Gibraltar later that day for survey and repairs, and four days later was able to proceed on her passage to the Clyde.

On the same day as this attack the Republican battleship *Jaime Primero* which was undergoing repairs at Carthagena was rocked by a serious explosion which wrecked the vessel. The explosion occurred while workmen were engaged in welding close to the magazine which was full of live shells. The casualty figures were 176 killed and about 200 injured, mostly serious.

Around that time a Republican submarine fired three torpedoes at the German cruiser *Leipzig* which all missed, as did the single torpedo fired in a later attack. This occurred just North of Oran.

Having been held at Ceuta for two months the Dutch steamer *Sarkani* was released minus her cargo and proceeded via Gibraltar to Rotterdam on June 21. It had been the Nationalists intention to keep this vessel and I believe they only let her go in recognition of the Dutch warship *Java's* evenhanded attitude in not opposing the vessels capture knowing that it had been loaded with munitions. An underwriters dream had come true.

The steamer *Dunavis* was seized in the Straits and taken into Ceuta where after examination she was released after a few hours and allowed to proceed.

On June 22 the Spanish steamer *Cabo Roche* escaped from Gibraltar where she had been under arrest and made it to nearby Algeciras a port held by the insurgents. The ship was held at Gibraltar following a claim by the Republic to take possession of her, the case going on since February. The watchman onboard had been overpowered and the vessel taken on behalf of its owner who was an insurgent sympathiser living at Seville, where she was subsequently taken and her cargo of cotton discharged.

It was reported that when the Russian steamer *Kuran* was captured by the cruiser *Almirante Cervera* while she was attempting to run the blockade at Almeria, she was carrying a cargo consisting of twenty aircraft, 44 tanks, 2,000 rifles, 1,000 machine guns, 2,000,000 cartridges and 400 tons of other war material.

*Author's Note*: Whilst acknowledging this report, during my research I have found no other evidence to corroborate this.

After the shelling of Valencia by German warships a great deal of unease was felt by the masters and crews of British merchant ships while lying at this port for some time to come. As a result at night some of the vessels took the precaution of going out of the harbour at night to where HMS *Shropshire* was anchored, and where they felt much safer.

The British trawler *Authorpe* was stopped off Valencia by the Italian flotilla leader *Giovanni di Verazzano*. An officer boarded her, but after examining her papers and conferring with the French Non-Intervention officer on board, allowed her to resume her voyage to the port.

At this time the steamers *Stancourt* and *Olavus* reported having passed floating mines off Cape Palos, on their way to Valencia. The latter vessel missed a mine by a few feet while the former passed close to two. As a result all British vessels sailing along the coast were ordered to keep beyond the 100 fathom limit, as it was considered that it was less dangerous of striking mines at such a distance from the shore.

On June 26 the Spanish motor vessel *Cabo Palos* was torpedoed and sunk by a submarine of unknown nationality off Punta Ifach, while on passage from Alicante to Valencia. This was actually 28 miles North of Alicante. Five of her crew were drowned and 45 including a woman who acted as nurse were successful in getting away in a lifeboat. Her master, Captain Manuel Hoyos, reported that he had observed a submarine in the vicinity, and gave instructions for the ship to change course, but the submarine had fired a torpedo which hit the ship in No. 3 hold and sank her within five minutes. Those in the lifeboat rowed for six hours before being picked up by the fishing vessel *Carmencita y Lolita* which took them to Alicante.

The Spanish sailing vessel *Trinidad* was intercepted by the Nationalist cruiser *Canarias* outside territorial waters, between Canet and Argeles, off the coast of Catalonia, while on passage from Sete to Port Vendres. The cruiser took the seven man crew prisoner, then towed the vessel further out to sea before sinking it with gunfire. Another sailing vessel, the *Carmelita* with a crew of ten which was in company with the *Trinidad* escaped and succeeded in making it to Port Vendres.

Having survived a shelling attack from the cruiser *Canarias*, off the Spanish coast, the Spanish oil tanker *Campero* in damaged condition managed to continue her voyage, but was then torpedoed by a submarine; the torpedo penetrated her empty oil tanks, but the ship remained afloat, and managed to reach Marseilles where she was found to have a 45ft hole in her starboard side.

Further vessels seized in the Straits of Gibraltar by Nationalist warships, taken into Ceuta, and later released with cargoes intact were the Greek *Varvara*, Russian *Dniestr*, Danish *Edith*, Danish *Dorrit* and the Latvian *Auseklis*.

On July 12 the Republican army tanker *Campilo* was being escorted by three warships from Carthagena to Valencia when the convoy was attacked by the Nationalist cruiser *Canarias*. No damage was done, the cruiser made off and the Republican vessels arrived at their destination.

A rare Republican success on that day was the capture of the insurgent motor vessel *Cala Mitjana* in the Straits of Gibraltar, which was normally controlled by the Nationalists. The Republican warship involved was the destroyer *Churruca*.

On July 15 the steamer *Lonia* was seized and taken to Palma, Majorca, by an insurgent warship, her cargo was confiscated and when released she made for Constantza.

On July 24 the Newport registered steamer *St. Quentin* was damaged while unloading at Valencia. The damage was not severe but water in No. 1 hold damaged about 200 tons of sugar. This vessel was managed by the B. & S. Shipping Co. Ltd., of Cardiff, and owned by the St. Quentin Steamship Co. Ltd., which was eventually to become the South American Saint Line.

On or about July 26 the Swedish steamer *Lola* put into Constantza, presumably for bunkers, enroute from Odessa. The Rumanian authorities suspected that she was carrying arms destined for Spain, and the allegation was that the cargo was actually incendiary bombs and explosives which were detailed in the Customs declaration as 'tinned fruit and vegetables'. At midnight the ship slipped out of port and chase was immediately given by a Rumanian destroyer which quickly overhauled her and brought her back to port.

Soon after the French steamer *Jacques Schiaffino* was attacked by a bi-plane 20 miles North-east of Minorca, but no damage occurred.

The Spanish steamer *Arichachu* which had left the Tyne for a Russian Black Sea port, while passing through the English Channel the master and four Spanish Fascists seized control of the ship and imprisoned the crew in the hold.

The Newport registered *"St. Quentin"* was bombed and damaged by aircraft at Valencia on July, 24, 1937.

*(York Collection)*

The ship was then brought into the Nationalist held port of Pasajes.

On July 29 the French motor vessel *Riri* which had been engaged in traffic between Alicante and Marseilles was captured by insurgent warships off the Catalan coast and taken to Majorca.

The Russian tanker *Varlaam Avanesov* was stopped by an armed trawler off Tangier and ordered to proceed to Ceuta, her second visit, where she was released after a delay of 6 hours.

On July 29 two Spanish tankers, the *Zorroza* and *Saustan* and the steamer *Andutz Mendi* which was escorting them were attacked by two submarines in French territorial waters near the Espiguette Lighthouse. The two tankers were able to make it to Marseilles whilst the cargo ship was badly damaged with great loss of life.

Senor Castel, master of the *Andutz Mendi* gave the following account of the incident:–

> We left Port Vendres at noon on Thursday in ballast for Marseilles with a crew of 31 men. We had reached a point about four miles from Espiguette, where we joined the *Saustan* and *Zorroza*, when suddenly two submarines surfaced on either side of us. Although it was clear weather we were unable to identify their nationality, and before I could hail the men on their decks a burst of machine-gun fire mowed down several of my crew. The rest got in a panic, some jumping overboard and others taking refuge in the holds. I stood on the poop utterly bewildered and helpless, since we were unarmed and could not defend ourselves. For about 45 minutes we were machine-gunned and shelled until the ship, now badly damaged, swung round out of control. Seeing that the position was hopeless, I called for a lifeboat to be lowered. We put out a fire which had broken out, and eight of us, myself, five officers and two seamen, got into the boat and began rowing towards land. The two submarines then made off and we managed to make our way to the shore.

The intervention by the French authorities and fishermen ensured that the vessel was saved and three days later she was brought into Sete. However the loss of 20 lives was a real tragedy.

The British Tanker Company's *British Corporal* Abadan for Land's End for orders with a cargo of benzine was attacked by three monoplane type heavy bombers about 30 miles West of Algiers. Thirty aerial bombs were dropped, and when the crew attempted to take to the boats the ship was machine-gunned. Damage was light and there were no casualties. The ship put back to Algiers.

On August 6 the Italian steamer *Mongioia* on passage from Italy for Spain to load cork for Philadelphia, was bombed by an aircraft 35 miles North of Algiers. Two bombs were dropped close to the ship causing serious injury to the master, and also causing a broken arm to the Non-Intervention Officer. In the attack the ship's plates were distorted, her rails twisted, and her hull and lifeboats holed. The wireless was wrecked, and shrapnel splinters fell all over the decks and in the cabins. In the engine-room the floor was torn up, the pipes burst and the engine wrenched from its rivets. The vessel put back for Algiers where the master was hospitalised.

On the same day, also off Algiers, the French steamer *Djebel Amour* was machine-gunned by an aircraft. There were no casualties. The vessel had been on passage from Oran. The Greek steamer *K. Ktistakis* was bombed 18 miles West of Algiers, but was undamaged. The vessel was on a voyage to Hamburg from Algiers.

On August 11 the Yugoslavian steamer *Plavnik* was taken to Melilla by an insurgent warship, but following examination was freed.

The Russian steamer *Dmitrov* was stopped in the Straits of Gibraltar and taken to Ceuta, but released after four hours.

On August 12 the Danish steamer *Edith* was bombed and sunk by insurgent aircraft about 30 miles South of Barcelona. The crew were rescued by two fishing boats which put out from Villaneuva y Geltru. The Nationalist account of the sinking is of particular interest:

> Machines from the air base in the Balearic Islands at midday yesterday, observed the steamer *Edith* bound for Tarragona. The vessel was flying the Danish flag and the special flag indicating the presence of a non-intervention control observer. The vessel was ordered by means of searchlight signals to make for Palma, Majorca. She did so, but later turned and made for Barcelona at full speed. The 'planes dropped 15-110lb bombs, two of which struck the vessel forward. The vessel caught fire and the crew abandoned her in two boats.

The Spanish Republican motor tanker *Campeador* was shelled and sunk 13 miles East of Kelibia, in position Lat 36.55N, Long.11.15E. with loss of twelve of her crew of 42. The British *Dido* rescuing three and the British *Clintonia* two survivors, all being landed at Tunis.

The crew accused Italian destroyers of having sunk the vessel off Kelibia, about sixty miles East of Tunis, yesterday. (30 survivors). The other twelve members of the crew were trapped in the engine-room and burned by blazing oil. The vessel was sunk by shells. The Spanish crew related that the Italian destroyer *Saetta* met the *Campeador* at 8am yesterday off Lampeduda Island, between Malta and the Tunisian coast; she followed the tanker's course, making circles round her. A second destroyer of the same type as the first but flying no flag and with her name painted out joined the *Saette* during the afternoon about sixty miles from Kelibia. The second destroyer followed them until it began to get dark. Then, as the destroyers did not show lights, the master of the tanker became uneasy. He headed for Kelibia, intending to seek shelter in that port, but the destroyers increased speed and headed him off. One of them fired a shell, which exploded in the engine-room, stopping the engines, and the vessel began to settle down by the stern. The crew began to lower their boats and before the boats reached the water two other shells struck the tanker. A fourth shell set fire to the oil, setting the whole vessel ablaze. The vessel, which had been carrying a cargo of 9,500 tons of petrol from Constantza to Valencia subsequently sank.

On August 14 the crews of French steamers in Tunis had a meeting to decide whether to refuse to sail unless they were given protection. The crew of the French cargo steamer *Parame*, which had arrived in Tunis after a narrow escape from being torpedoed, had called the meeting. The master of the *Parame* had reported on his arrival from Marseilles that a submarine had fired a torpedo at this vessel 20 miles off Bizerta. The torpedo exploded 150 yards away from the vessel. The *Parame* had wirelessed the news of the attack to Bizerta and had expected an escort to convoy her but none arrived.

On the same day the Panamanian motor tanker *Geo. W. McKnight* was shelled and set on fire by several destroyers and a submarine. Clearly now the Italians were openly assisting the Nationalists at sea as well as on land. This attack occurred 11 miles North of Zembra Island. The British tanker *British Commodore* picked up the crew of 38, all German except one American. Eventually the British tanker took her in tow and with assistance of an Italian tug *Hercule* brought her, with fire now extinguished into a safe anchorage off Tunis. Subsequently the ship was taken to Bizerta where most of her crude oil cargo was transferred to the *British Commodore*. The *Geo. W. McKnight* was owned by the American Standard Oil Company, who also owned the cargo.

On August 17 the Spanish steamer *Conde de Abasolo* was torpedoed and sunk by an Italian destroyer off the Italian island of Pantellaria, while on a voyage to the Black Sea via Malta. The torpedo had hit the vessel in the engine-room killing several of the crew. The British *City of Wellington* picked up the 23 survivors.

Another Spanish steamer sunk at about this time, that being the *Ciudad de Cadiz*, which was attacked by the insurgent submarine *C3* 15 miles off Bozcaada. The submarine fired eight rounds and launched two torpedoes and the merchant ship sank in 40 minutes. Three boats were launched with 75 crew and four jumped overboard. All were saved by the Russian tanker *Varlaam Avanesov* and taken to Istanbul.

At about this time the steamer *Aldecoa* took refuge in the port of Algiers, after being pursued by an Italian destroyer.

On August 18 the Spanish steamer *Armuru* bound West, with a cargo of wheat from Odessa for Spain was torpedoed by an unknown submarine in the neighbourhood of Bozcaada. The vessel managed to reach the shore and was beached in a sinking condition. The crew were rescued by a Turkish steamer; there were no casualties. The vessel was subsequently declared a total loss. As a result of this and other earlier attacks in this vicinity the Spanish Government Charge d'Affaires at Angora asked for the protection of the Turkish Navy in this area.

The British steamer *Noemijulia* carrying a cargo of iron ore and phosphate from Marseilles for Spain was attacked by aircraft in the vicinity of Port Vendres. The master described the aircraft as having number and marks – '528' and '529' and black circle with white crosses and two white bars. None of the bombs dropped hit their intended target and the vessel made for the safety of Port Vendres.

On August 30 the Spanish steamer *Ciutat de Reus* put into Port Vendres following an attack on her by an insurgent submarine. Four shells missed but a fifth hit the vessel's waterline. There were no casualties.

The Greek owned tanker *Romford* which was sailing under the British flag from Barcelona to Constantza was attacked by aircraft when about 20 miles off Barcelona. The five bombs dropped fell 50 yards from the ship which escaped damage. Thereafter the vessel put into Marseilles where the master reported the incident.

On August 31 the Russian motor vessel *Timiriazev* bound from Cardiff for Port Said with a cargo of coal, was torpedoed by a submarine 60 miles East of Algiers, and soon foundered. Her crew of 26 men and three women were rescued by an Algerian fishing vessel.

The Greek steamer *Aikaterini T*, Makri for Norway, was forced to enter Palma for examination, but soon after the Nationalists allowed her to proceed.

After an unsuccessful attack with torpedoes from a submarine on HMS *Havock* in the Mediterranean, the vessel counter-attacked with depth charges. The identity of the assailant was unknown.

On September 2 the British tanker *Woodford* was attacked by a submarine (obviously Italian) on the surface, which torpedoed and sank her in international waters whilst she was on route to Valencia with 10,000 tons of petrol from Constantza. Of her crew, all were Greek, with the exception of a Hungarian radio operator, a Rumanian cook and a British control officer. Eight members of the crew were injured and one killed.

On the same day the British tanker *Burlington* was captured by an insurgent warship and taken into Palma, where her cargo of 7,700 tons of oil bound from Batum to Carthagena was confiscated.

The capture of the *Burlington* had taken place off the island of Skyros. At the same time and just within sight of it, the Russian steamer *Blagoev* bound from Russia for France with a cargo of Asphalt (pitch), was stopped by a submarine which fired a warning shot. The crew were ordered to take to the boats, and then the vessel was torpedoed and sunk. One of the Russian sailors was killed by debris from the explosion. The remainder of the crew safely reached land at Kymi, Euboea.

Meanwhile in the Straits of Gibraltar further ships were being stopped and taken under force of arms to Ceuta for examination, but quickly released. These included the Swedish *Bernicia* and Greek tanker *Katerina*. The tanker *Romford* which had survived an attack less than two weeks ago off Barcelona was captured off Algiers by the cruiser *Canarias* and taken into Ceuta. This vessel had until recently been the Greek *Ionia* and had not been flying the British flag for long. She was released a day later, apparently with her cargo of oil intact, and made for Land's End for orders. Laden tankers were often to make for Land's End, as when they had left their loading port their destination in Europe had yet to be decided, and on or before their arrival off Cornwall this had been determined.

The steamer *Jenny* with a provisional British registration was stopped in the Straits and ordered into Gibraltar where the authorities made an extensive examination of her cargo. After eight days she proceeded, but by now was the *River Dart*.

On September 6 the British tanker *Pegasus* was stopped off Cape Sigri, by a submarine which fired a warning shot. The vessel hove to, but a further shot was fired, and the master thereupon hoisted the signal 'I am stopped'. The submarine which was about 150 yards distant hoisted the Spanish Nationalist flag, and then sailed away in a Westerly direction, without examining or bothering the merchant ship any further. The *Pegasus* carrying 4,500 kilos of keresene continued her voyage calling at Alexandria, but thereafter made for her discharge port, Constantza.

Two British steamers were damaged by an air attack on Valencia on the night of September 15. These were the *Pracat* and the *Jean Weems*. The latter ship was the worst affected, one member of crew killed and the master, Captain Eversett had a wound to his thigh. This vessel was badly damaged: which was extensive to shell plating on the port side, superstructure and bridge.

The Nationalist cruiser *Canarias* attacked a convoy of two Spanish merchant ships, the *Rey Jamie II* and *J.J. Sister* which were being escorted by three Republican destroyers from Barcelona with arms and foodstuffs for Port Mahon, the Republican Naval base in Minorca, which was the only one of the Balearic Islands to remain loyal to the Republic. After an hours battle the destroyers made off, more or less, undamaged, and the cruiser thereafter brought the two captured merchant ships into Palma.

The Panamanian steamer *Adria* bound from Swansea for Genoa with a cargo of coal was stopped in the Straits and taken into Ceuta. All the ship's papers were examined, and as she was not proceeding to or from a Spanish port she was allowed to leave after 16 hours detention. Other ships so treated in this period were the Danish *Tula*, Egyptian *Reefer* and *Emilie Maersk*.

In a further air attack on Valencia the Spanish steamer *Guecho* was badly hit with bombs and lay with her stern on the bottom and a heavy list to port, her after deck actually being under water.

On September 23 at dawn the port of Tarragona was bombed by three Italian Savoia-Marchetti aircraft, which damaged two British ships in port, the *Hamsterley* and the *Sheaf Spear* recently acquired by Jack Billmeir's Stanhope Steamship Company. The damage was not too serious, but a number of cases of shock were reported among both crews.

After ten months detention, the master and nine seamen from the captured Russian steamer *Komsomol* were released and passed through France on their way back to Russia. The remainder of the crew – seventeen were at that time still held in prison in Tolosa, but soon followed.

Early in October HMS *Basilisk* while on patrol in the Western Mediterranean was attacked by an unknown submarine. One torpedo was fired at the vessel, which retaliated by dropping a depth charge, the result of which was unknown.

The *Cervantes*, owned by MacAndrews & Co. Ltd., of London, who operated a liner service between the United Kingdom and Mediterranean ports was making for Tarragona on October 8, when she was attacked by an insurgent aircraft when eight miles from the port. Although undamaged the ship had to alter course to seaward, but eventually returned to Valencia.

During that same day two air attacks by Republican aircraft on Palma resulted on one bomb falling near the British Consulate, another fell about 300 yards from the cruiser HMS *Delhi* which was anchored off the port. No damage was sustained.

The French cargo steamer *Cassidaigne* was captured by four Italian warships off Majorca; she was on passage from Marseilles to Oran. She was forced to enter Palma, where Spanish Fascists tried to get him to land his cargo of empty casks, but he refused. The French and Danish Consuls intervened and obtained the release of the vessel just as the French destroyer *Le Fantasque* arrived to convoy her towards Oran.

On October 12 the Spanish motor vessel *Cabo Santo Tome* which was carrying a cargo of aircraft and 1,800 tons of war material from Russia, was intercepted by two insurgent warships 45 miles off the Algerian coast, between Cap de Garde and Cap Rosa. She was shelled, but being armed herself with four 57mm guns and four 45mm guns as well as anti-aircraft guns the merchant ship returned their fire. To no avail, the merchant ship was struck in the stern and caught fire. The master succeeded in beaching her three miles from Cap Rosa but thereafter she exploded and sank deeper in the water. One member of crew was killed and six wounded.

On October 31 the Greek steamer *Zephyros* was stopped in the Straits of Gibraltar and taken into Ceuta for examination.

The British steamer *Jean Weems* was attacked and sunk by insurgent aircraft 16 miles from Cape San Sebastian, while on passage from Marseilles to Barcelona with a cargo of condensed milk and wheat. There were no casualties among her crew of 16 and two Non-Intervention Control Officers, who after almost seven hours in a boat landed on the Catalan coast.

The Royal Navy were very concerned to be seen doing their duty properly. For some time past they had suspected that British ships were on occasions carrying war materials to the Republic in direct contravention of the Merchant Shipping (Carriage of Munitions to Spain) Act, 1936. As a result on occasions British ships were taken into port and examined in detail. One such ship to be examined was the Cardiff managed steamer *African Mariner* which was intercepted in the Eastern Mediterranean whilst bound from Odessa and Novorossisk to Barcelona. The Admiralty had suspected for some time that the owners of this ship were engaged in gun-running, and had watched her movements with great attention. Having been stopped by HMS *Greyhound* an armed guard was put on board and the vessel escorted into Valletta Harbour, Malta, arriving on November 19.

Much of the *African Mariner's* cargo of salt fish and sulphate of ammonia was discharged, but rods were used to probe the wheat in her deep holds. After ten days of exhaustive searching by the Naval Authorities in Malta nothing was found and the vessel was allowed to sail with her much needed cargo, and subsequently arrived at Barcelona.

The same procedure was adopted by the Royal Navy in respect of the British steamer *Euphorbia* which was intercepted in Spanish waters on November 21 by HMS *Galatea* and brought into Gibraltar with an armed guard on board. The master stated that he was on a voyage from Odessa, Poti and Istanbul to Gdynia with a cargo of Manganese ore and cotton. On examination of the ship's documents and cargo it was clearly found that she was not in fact contravening the Merchant Shipping Act, and indeed not bound for Spain, and after 24 hours the Armed Naval Guard was withdrawn. Having taken on bunkers she continued her voyage.

The confiscated steamers *Janu* (Panamanian), *Nagos* (Greek), *Gardelaki* (Greek) and *Alix* (Norwegian) which had originally been taken to Ceuta, were now being used in the service of the Nationalist authorities, with a Spanish master and crews.

Further vessels were detained in the Straits and taken to Ceuta for examination, and were all subsequently released accounted for – Swedish *Valencia*, Russian *Zurupa* towing tugs *Valero Tchkaloff* and *Aleksander Dokov*, Danish *Margrete*, Polish *Lechistan*, Danish *Chr. Sass*, French *Sydney*, French *Francois* (with a heavy list), Norwegian *Breidablik*, Danish *Charkow*, Norwegian *Felix*, and the Russian *Stchors*. As can be seen some of these ships had been in Ceuta before.

On December 27 the French steamer *Yolande* on passage from Marseilles to Barcelona was intercepted by the Nationalist cruisers *Canarias* and *Almirante Cervera*. The merchant ship gave out a distress call which was answered by the French destroyer *Vauquelin*. The cruisers allegation that the *Yolande* was carrying arms was taken seriously and the French warship undertook that the vessel would be examined thoroughly, but in a French port. As a result the French warship brought the *Yolande* into Port Vendres where the Custom House authorities examined the ship's papers and cargo, and it was found to be 500 tons of tobacco and 400 tons of beans. The matter was closed.

Late in December that veteran of the Spanish Civil War, the Newport steamer *Bramhill* was lying at Burriana when the Nationalist Navy shelled the port. Several shells hit the Welsh ship but amazingly little damage was caused and no injuries suffered by the crew. The *Bramhill* left port for Marseilles where she was examined and a report passed to Claude Angel, but repairs were deferred until a later more convenient time.

Following the release of the steamer *Seven Seas Spray* by Franco's forces at Santona on November 1, 1937 Alfred Pope decided to rename the ship before sending her back to the Spanish war zone. As a result she was given the new name of *Seabank Spray* appropriately reflecting his interest in the Porthcawl hotel. On January 16th, 1938 the ship was lying at Burriana when three insurgent aircraft attacked the port, and a bomb fell within 200 yards of the vessel. The ship's luck continued to hold out as again she suffered only very minor damage.

The Dutch steamer *Hannah* was torpedoed and sunk seven miles off Cape San Antonio, fortunately without casualties, the crew landing at Javea.

Further detentions and releases at Ceuta accounted for the Greek *Athinai*, Russian *Petrovsky*, Greek *Aikaterini T*, Greek *Meropi*, Panamanian *Norse Carrier* and the Estonian *Juss* and *Pomaron*, which both had their cargoes of coal on route to Barcelona and Valencia respectively confiscated.

The American tanker *Nantucket Chief* carrying a cargo of petrol and kerosene was on her way from Russia to Barcelona when captured by insurgent warships and taken to Palma. Representations by the United States Government for the release of the vessel were agreed, but only after the ship had delivered her precious cargo to a Nationalist held mainland port. Sure enough she turned up at Gibraltar in ballast some time later with a very disgruntled crew who would only agree to sail the vessel to Texas when their wages had been assured.

On January 20 the British steamer *Thorpeness* was damaged by an air attack while lying at Tarragona which killed seven members of the crew and wounded seven others who were taken to hospital. Some of her plates were stove in, her foredeck plating was damaged and temporary repairs had to be made before she was allowed to proceed to Barcelona to complete the discharge of her cargo.

Four days later the French steamer *Prado* was captured by an insurgent warship which ordered her to follow it, but a distress call was answered by the French destroyer *Albatros* which rescued her.

Two torpedoes were fired at the British steamer *Clonlara* when the vessel was 10 miles off Sagunto. Both missed and the ship proceeded to Burriana. Another British ship was to share the same good fortune, that was the *Lake Geneva* which was attacked off Valencia, but on this occasion the torpedo actually passed under the vessel.

On January 26 the British steamer *Sheaf Crest* had just left Gibraltar bound for Spanish ports when she was intercepted by an insurgent vessel which ordered her back to that port. Her master refused and his wireless message for assistance was answered by the destroyer HMS *Boreas* which intervened, and the vessel proceeded without further interruption.

On that same day Captain Arnold Crone, master of the British steamer *Dover Abbey* met his death in an insurgent air raid on Valencia, in which 125 people were killed and 208 wounded. Captain Crone was ashore at the time, as the ship was not hit. At the time she was loading oranges.

The Danish steamer *Gyda* and the Russian *Igarka* were stopped in the Straits and taken to Ceuta, but both freed after a short delay.

On January 31 the British steamer *Endymion* was torpedoed and sunk in the Mediterranean by what was believed to be an Italian submarine. There was outrage felt in Britain and Spain at the heavy loss of life, which accounted for eleven people, including the master, his wife and the 2nd engineer. As a result of the quick action of the Republican authorities the remaining members of the crew were speedily rescued. The Royal Navy stepped up their patrols following this incident.

On February 4 the British steamer *Alcira* was bombed and sunk 20 miles from Barcelona by two insurgent seaplanes. She sank immediately, but her crew of 25 and non-intervention control officer were saved. As a result HMS *Newcastle* arrived at Barcelona to investigate the sinking and thereafter conveyed the crew to Marseilles.

The French steamer *El Mansour* had left Port Vendres for Algiers with 150 passengers when she was followed by Nationalist warships on February 18. A shell was fired which landed about 200 yards from the vessel. A wireless message to the French Navy for assistance was answered by the destroyer *La Palme* who intervened and escorted the merchant ship for the rest of her voyage to Algiers.

A month after her last incident with the insurgents, on February 22 the French steamer *Prada* was attacked and machine-gunned by an insurgent aircraft 12 miles off Valencia. One member of the crew was wounded. The French destroyer *Epervier* was sent to investigate and render assistance to the ship which was slightly damaged.

Claude Angel's steamer *Bramden* was lying at Sagunto on February 25 when six insurgent seaplanes made a determined attack on the vessel in the port. One bomb actually landed on the ship's oiltank but fortunately failed to explode. Three members of her crew including the wireless operator, Mr. G. Garrod, were wounded by shrapnel, but thankfully none seriously.

At about the same time the British steamer *Shetland* was damaged by bombing at the same port, but made for Valencia for repairs and survey.

During February, 1938 the following neutral vessels were stopped in the Straits of Gibraltar or in other areas of the Mediterranean and taken into insurgent ports for examination. Russian *Menjinski* (Ceuta), Panamanian *Yolanda* (Palma), Finnish *Britannic* (Ceuta), *Veli Ragnar* of Lovisa (Ceuta), Swedish *Vikingland* (Ceuta), Russian *Lunacharski* (Ceuta).

On March 6 a sea battle occurred around 70 miles off Cape Palos between Republican and Nationalist warships, Spaniard against Spaniard. The identity of all the vessels engaged in the battle is not known to me, but the Nationalist (insurgent) cruisers *Canarias, Baleares* and *Almirante Cervera* were, as was the Republican destroyers *Sanchez Barcaiztequi, Almirante Antequera* and *Lepanto*. A torpedo from a destroyer hit the cruiser *Baleares* with devasting effect, and with wave upon wave of Republican air attacks concentrating on the damaged vessel the cruiser was disabled and sank with a heavy loss of life. The Royal Navy, not too far off, intervened to save as many of the crew of the stricken vessel as possible, namely HMS *Kempenfelt* and HMS *Boreas,* but the air attacks were continuous and whilst none was aimed at the Royal Navy, nonetheless a member of the crew of HMS *Boreas* was killed by bomb splinters and three others wounded.

The following day HMS *Blanche* and HMS *Brilliant* which were engaged on patrol duties were attacked by five aircraft between Alicante and Gibraltar. There were no casualties in the attack and no hits were recorded.

The British steamer *Maryad* was slightly damaged at Alicante during an air attack. There were no casualties.

Support for the Republican cause had come mainly from the Russians and ever since the war had started they had been sending supplies, both war materials, fuel and foodstuffs, much of which had been consigned in their own ships. The Russians had suffered heavy casualties at the hands of the Nationalist forces, with many of their vessels being sunk, damaged, captured and confiscated. From the start of 1938 the Russians declared to the Republican Government that whilst prepared to provide the supplies she needed, they were no longer willing to risk their own merchant ships. Therefore, if the Republicans wanted the supplies they would have to send their own ships to fetch them.

The main route for supplies reaching Spain from Russia was from Odessa in the Black Sea to the Mediterranean held ports. As the result of this ultimatum by Russia, the Republican Government set about chartering vessels to undertake what was clearly a hazardous voyage. Jack Billmeir was heavily involved with the supply of the Republican side, and when asked to help, felt obliged to risk his ships on the run.

Consequently, it was no surprise when it was reported that the Billmeir steamer *Stanbrook* had left Malta on January 24, 1938 en route for Odessa in ballast. Franco knew what was going on and so did the Royal Navy. The Nationalists had intensified their campaign against Merchant ships in the Mediterranean and the Royal Navy in an attempt to be seen to be doing their duty in an impartial way had already started checking cargoes of British ships to ensure if possible that no war materials and arms were carried in ships flying the British flag.

At this time a number of incidents occurred in the Mediterranean involving British ships. A number of merchant vessels had actually been torpedoed and sunk by submarines, suspected then and later proved to be Italian. The Italians had consistently supported Franco's forces throughout the conflict, and attacks at sea by submarines only ended after a stern warning by the Royal Navy that any unidentified submarine found in the Mediterranean would be sunk without warning.

On occasions a Spanish merchant ship would make for a neutral North African port where her cargo destined for Republican Spain was transhipped into vessels of other nationalities for the short dash across to Spain. On March 1, 1938 Lloyds reported that Billmeir's steamer *Stanbrook*, fresh from her voyage from Odessa to Spain, was taking the cargo of the Spanish steamer *Escolano* which had put into Bona harbour. Thereafter the British ship delivered the precious goods to the Spanish.

During February, 1938 the tanker *Stanmount* was lying at Valencia when the crew learned of Billmeir's intention of sending the vessel to the Black Sea to load at Odessa. They promptly went on strike, demanding a further 50 per cent increase in the danger rates of pay for the Spanish war zone. Eventually Captain John Roberts, her master, was able to make for Malta where they arrived on February 27. At this port the crew, having refused to continue their voyage to the Black Sea were paid off at their own request. They were repatriated to the United Kingdom at their own expense and the ship then signed on a Maltese crew for the remainder of the voyage.

On February 27 the Billmeir steamer *Stanwell* arrived at Tarragona with a cargo of 8,000 tons of coal from Newport, Monmouthshire, and was moored alongside the quay forming the southern arm of the inner harbour. At 4.30am on March 15 an air attack was carried out by an insurgent seaplane, flying at a height of about 300 feet. The *Stanwell* was obviously the target, as two bombs were dropped on the deck of the vessel, the first bomb dropped on the port side of the saloon, carrying away the bulwarks, iron decks, both main and 'tweendeck. The saloon and bridge then burst into flames. Steam was raised immediately and hoses connected, but the water service pipes were useless owing to the damage. The fire spread to the bunker coal. The fire brigade arrived and by 7am the fire was under control. The master, chief officer, chief steward and the non-intervention officer were sleeping in the saloon at the time. Captain Davies of Cardiff, the master, gave orders for all hands to abandon ship owing to the fire. The second bomb was dropped on the port side after end of the firemen's forecastle, carrying away bulwarks and decks, both main and 'tweendeck, in No. 1 hold, and fracturing the vessel's side with a V-shaped crack from the main deck to a depth of 22 feet. The firemen's forecastle was completely gutted on the port side and the ship's side was pushed outward steampipes were torn away and No. 1 hatch coamings flattened out.

During this period the wounded were carried ashore to the hospital. As a result of the attack, two men Messrs Mulholland and King, firemen, both from Newport were killed, as was the Danish Non-Intervention Control Officer. Four other members of the crew were seriously injured. The chief officer and chief steward were also slightly injured. Temporary repairs had to be effected before the ship could be towed from the port to be repaired. The crew were housed ashore after the attack as the accommodation was destroyed. They refused to reboard the vessel and demanded repatriation home.

This was one of many attacks being carried out by aircraft. Clearly they were designed to hamper supplies to Republican ports, by dissuading owners from sending their ships into ports where considerable danger existed, and to interrupt the actual cargo working on the ships themselves. The insurgents felt that the disabling of a ship was a bonus which obviously supported the main objective.

An air attack on March 12 on Carthagena by Nationalist aircraft was to severely damage the Republican cruisers,

of HM Dockyard, where her cargo was discharged and examined. It was found that she was carrying cartridge cases, aeroplane engines and other articles of war.

Billmeir was horrified when he heard that his vessel had been detained, and on hearing that his master had been charged before the Police Court at Gibraltar with the offence of 'taking and carrying munitions of war to Spain', and granted bail of £100 with two sureties in the same sum, he immediately despatched Mr. D.N. Pritt, KC., MP. to defend him.

Meanwhile the cargo of the *Stancroft* of which 95 per cent was not of articles of war, was restowed in the vessel, with the exception of the munitions. A new master, Captain S.L. Spence arrived in Gibraltar to take over command, and later the ship was allowed to leave making straight for Valencia.

The Republican Government then made a formal complaint to the British Government that the cargo on board the vessel, including the war equipment was their property and by ordering the vessel out of Valencia, had indeed been seized on Spanish territory. A claim was made for the seized cargo to be returned. The complaint, however, fell on deaf ears.

The trial against Captain Scott proceeded, and evidence was given for the prosecution by the Non-Intervention Control Observer and the ship's Second Officer to the effect that the Master was privy to the munitions being on board. However the defence made the submission that there was no case to answer on the following grounds:–

(1) No evidence of goods going to Valencia.
(2) Goods conveyed between Spanish ports not subject to Non-Intervention Agreement.
(3) Master not privy to contraband on board.
(4) Charge discloses no offence.

Counsel for the Crown replied that goods and munitions carried to Spanish ports came under the Act, also that the master was privy to carriage of prohibited goods.

However, the Court decided that there was no case to answer on the grounds that the prohibited articles were being conveyed from one Spanish port to another, and Captain Scott was discharged, with no order made as to costs. Billmeir was jubilant.

During an air attack on Barcelona on May 12 two ships were damaged, the Pelton Steamship Company's *Zelo* suffered one member of her crew critically injured when a bomb fell on the quay, twenty yards from the ship. The *African Mariner* was moored next to the *Zelo*, and a Greek galley boy was slightly injured in the face by small fragments of shrapnel. Damage to the Welsh ship was confined to the wireless operator's cabin, the wireless aerial was cut down from the mast and she received three large holes in her funnel.

Shortly after, Claude Angel's by now famous ship, the *Yorkbrook* was damaged at Valencia when a bomb fell on the quay near her. There were no casualties on board, although her bridge and lifeboats were slightly damaged. She was

The Pelton Steamship Company's steamer *Zelo* was damaged by an air attack on Barcelona on May 12.
*(Laurence Dunn)*

The Barry Shipping Company's *St. Winifred* on May 22 at Alicante was damaged by an air attack. Subsequently on June 6 in another attack five members of crew were killed.

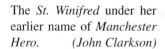

The *St. Winifred* under her earlier name of *Manchester Hero.* (John Clarkson)

however, able to proceed without making repairs.

On May 22 the Barry Shipping Company's (later to become the South American Saint Line) steamer *St. Winifred* was bombed and damaged at Alicante whilst unloading a cargo of foodstuffs. There were no casualties at that time and the damage to the ship was reported by her master as:–

> Main condenser inlet and fresh-water distiller fractured, starboard side engine-room deckhouse, port side poop deckhouse, fiddley deck, all bridges, decks sprung, boats concussion strained, starboard boat holed, all inside accommodation woodwork amidships broken, bridges woodwork shattered, telegraph, electric lights, wireless damaged, shrapnel perforations over all, much smaller damage, wood fiddley deckhouse shattered, fresh water tank damaged. Can effect temporary repairs.

However, she was not so fortunate on June 6, as during two insurgent air attacks on Alicante she was so badly damaged that she was in danger of sinking. In these attacks five crew members were killed, Engineer Halliday, Seamen Hennessey and McMillan, the messroom boy and the cabin boy. As a result she was eventually towed to Marseilles

The British flag tanker *English Tanker* was bombed and sunk at Alicante on June 6. This ship although registered at Newcastle was in fact owned in Spain

*(Laurence Dunn collection)*

The Llanelli registered *Isadora* was bombed and sunk at Castellon on June 9, just six days before the city fell to the Nationalists.

*(Laurence Dunn)*

where she was subsequently declared a constructive total loss, and in November was sold to Italians who after carrying out repairs placed her into service as the *Capo Vita*. Richard Street, the managing director of the owners was so sickened by this casualty that he immediately withdrew from the Spanish trade.

The Welsh managed steamer *Penthames* was lying at Valencia towards the end of May when she was the subject of a number of air attacks. On the 20th four bombs landed near the ship, but damage was slight. Two days later she received a direct hit during another raid. The master Captain Cochrane and second mate were interviewed by reporters:–

> Captain Cochrane alleges that the 'planes bore German markings, and he added that a telegram of protest had been sent to London. He recalled that on the previous Friday (May 20) four bombs had burst in the vicinity of the vessel. Mr. Brown, one of the officers stated that three bombs were dropped and that in his opinion, the vessel was aimed at. Two bombs, he said, burst 45 feet from the vessel, and the third struck the deck, making an enormous hole and destroying the cabins of the officers and engineers. Two officers, Graham and Oglesberg, received a number of wounds, and a Chinese boy had his legs torn and his shoulder dislocated. A fire broke out in the vessel but was rapidly got under control by the crew and the harbour officials.

The ship was again to be the subject of air attacks on May 25 and 31, and as a result of the latter she sank at her moorings in the port. Fortunately no one had lost his life, although the attacks had been heavy. During the attack on Valencia on May 25 our old friend the *Thorpehall* was caught at anchor just outside the port and was sunk by the insurgent attack. Of her crew five were wounded including three who lived at Cardiff.

Three days later the British steamer *Greatend* was bombed and sunk at her moorings whilst lying at Valencia. The Mooringwell Steamship Company's ship *Jeanne M* was moored at the Coal Quay at Barcelona on May 29 when she was damaged by bomb splinters and concussion from an air attack on the port. The ship suffered damage to her hull and superstructure which was subsequently repaired at Barry. At the time of the attack she was discharging a cargo of coal and generals from South Wales.

On June 6 the British *English Tanker* was sunk by bombs at Alicante. After the war was over she was refloated and repaired by the Spanish. The Stone & Rolfe steamer *Isadora* was badly damaged by an attack at Castellon at 1am on June 9, just six days before the fall of the port to the Nationalists, when three bombs struck the vessel. Damage consisted of her bridge, cabins and engine room being wrecked and the following day the ship sank. There were fortunately no casualties in the attack. At the time she had been unloading a badly needed cargo of wheat which she had brought from Marseilles.

After taking Castellon, the insurgents subsequently raised the *Isadora* and after repairing the ship placed her under their own flag under the new name of *Castillo Frias*. Prior to the fall of the port her crew had been conveyed from the war zone by the Royal Navy.

On the same day as the Llanelli steamer was sunk at Castellon, the Billmeir steamer *Stanray* whilst proceeding towards Valencia was attacked at 2am off Gandia by a seaplane which machine-gunned her. The aircraft circled her twice and poured a stream of bullets at her, but fortunately her aim was bad and no harm was done by the attack. The ship arrived at Valencia on the morning of June 10 without further incident.

Since the division of Republican territory, and the increase in insurgent attacks, many owners were not prepared to risk their ships in the war zone. As a result cargoes were being transhipped at Marseilles and Oran, into vessels that were prepared to run the risk and take the much needed cargoes into Republican Spain. In the main these ships were British, and as can be imagined they were handsomely rewarded, although the instances of damage and loss were far more numerous than had previously been the case.

## Chapter 8
# FREDERICK JONES AND COMPANY

Frederick Jones, owner of the Abbey Line, seen as a young man. *(Welsh Industrial & Maritime Museum)*

In relation to the Civil War British shipowners were actually earning enhanced freight rates to engage in the trade. After almost fifteen years of continuously depressed freight rates, it was difficult to keep out of a trade which was likely to yield some handsome returns. Many historians have asserted that owners were earning double their normal profits. I contend that this is not so, they were actually earning something like double their gross freight. Simply defined this meant that a profit of say £200 on a freight of £2,500 prior to the civil war or on a voyage not connected with the trade, returned on a voyage to or from Spain during the conflict something like £2,700 on a gross freight of £5,000. Clearly the returns were very good. The expenses of running to Spain were greater than other trades, but this was only marginally so, and usually related to war risk and increased crew insurance and to crew war bonuses. This left considerable profit for the owner prepared to enter into the trade. Whilst owners were prepared to risk their ships it is clear that seafarers were also prepared to take the risks associated with the trade, and who could blame them after such unemployment as was experienced in the depression of the early 1930s.

Many commentators have asserted that usually old ships were employed in the trade thus leaving greater profits for owners. This is partly true, old ships were used mostly, but that was because of the war risks insurance which on an old ship with low capital value was fairly reasonable. However, the employment of new tonnage which incurred the penalty of high insurance premiums was entirely prohibitive to owners. The only gains therefore were to be found by using older tonnage.

In my book *The Abbey Line* (1983) I included a chapter on the Spanish Civil War, and because this is the only company of which I have a detailed account of each vessel's voyages and earnings, and its historical importance I quote from it at length.

In consequence of Frederick Jones' decision to enter this trade, the *Neath Abbey* was chartered to the Nederlandsch Bevrachtings Hantoor and loaded foodstuffs at Rotterdam commencing on April 8, 1937 the freight for this was £3,612 12s 1d and whilst on voyage charters payment was usually made on discharge of the cargo, Frederick Jones had no experience of this trade or the charterers, and before agreeing to carry this cargo insisted that payment was made in advance on completion of loading. For this purpose his younger son, Herbert Stanley Jones went to Rotterdam to receive the payment. The ship thereafter sailed and completed discharge at Alicante on May 1. The profit made on the voyage outwards was £2,369 3s 5d and represented what the ship had previously taken over a year to earn. At noon on May 1 a freight was accepted for the ship, and she proceeded in

The Abbey Line steamer *Neath Abbey* earned considerable freights during the Spanish Civil War.

ballast from Alicante to Valencia where she commenced loading fruit on behalf of the Golden Cross Line. This cargo was completed by moving around the coast and taking on further parcels of fruit at Castellon and Burriana before she set out for Liverpool where on discharge being completed she proceeded in ballast to Port Talbot where she arrived on May 22, the freight for this homeward passage had been £2,481 yielding a profit of £1,664 19s 2d.

The steamer *Melrose Abbey* had carried a cargo of pyrites from the Nationalist held port of Huelva to Dublin in April, 1937. On completion of discharge she ballasted across to Rotterdam where her next voyage was to be for the Republican side.

On May 2, 1937 the *Melrose Abbey*, not a year old, commenced loading foodstuffs at Rotterdam for Valencia on behalf of the Lamorna Shipping Co. Ltd at a freight of £4,100. On arrival at Valencia the ship was delayed before her cargo could be unloaded and as a result demurrage for 4 days three hours was paid to the firm at £50 per day, ie £206 5s 0d. The ship then proceeded in ballast to Sfax where a cargo of phosphate, not connected with the Spanish trade was loaded at a freight of £2,441 14s 4d for Rotterdam.

On May 23 the *Neath Abbey* commenced loading coal at Port Talbot for the Lamorna Shipping Co. Ltd which was destined for Carthagena, the freight involved was £4,313 12s 10d and on entering the Mediterranean the ship had to call at Gibraltar to collect representatives of the Non-Intervention Committee for which purpose the firm was refunded £6 2s 6d port charges, thereafter the ship discharged at Carthagena and proceeded to Sfax where she loaded phosphate at a freight of £2,511 4s 8d for Nantes. She then proceeded to Flushing for bunkers, arriving on July 16.

On June 20 the *Melrose Abbey* commenced loading another cargo of foodstuffs at Rotterdam for the Nederlandsh Bevrachtings Hantoor for a £4,698 1s 11d freight destined for Alicante and on discharge proceeded in ballast to Phillipville (French North Africa) where iron ore was loaded for Grangemouth (freight £2,423 7s 5d) and after unloading she went in ballast to Immingham, arriving on August 8.

The Spanish (Republican) Authorities were having difficulties in obtaining woodpulp in which to pack fruit for export abroad, and as this fruit represented a major part of the economy, they tackled the search for pulp with some urgency. As a result on July 17 Herbert Stanley Jones was sent by his father to join the *Neath Abbey* at Flushing, and with him on board the ship passed through the Kiel Canal out into the Baltic, and then anchored at Hernosand in Sweden.

The master of the *Neath Abbey* was a fluent Welsh speaker named Jones, and everyone on board the vessel were surprised when the Pilot for the passage through the Kiel Canal conversed with him in Welsh. This was due to the fact that in Germany at that time it was a condition that before qualifying all master mariners had to have some experience under sail, and the Pilot had obtained part of his by sailing on a Cardigan ketch. Returning to the voyage:–

At this time he (H.S. Jones) was in conversation with the Spanish Commercial Attache in Sweden and a Swedish National – Mr Axel J. Ahlstrand and negotiated a freight for a cargo of woodpulp from the Swedish Mills at Utansjo and Bollsta destined for Valencia of £6,859 (profit £4,937 15s 8d). At this time it was arranged for the ship to be taken on time-charter to the Spanish Government directly, on her return from the Mediterranean. The *Neath Abbey* proceeded to Valencia without incident and quickly unloaded and then proceeded to Bona to load a part cargo of iron ore, completing at Bizerta, and then set off for Middlesbrough where her cargo was discharged on behalf of Scott Bros. Ltd at a freight of £2,626 5s 3d.

On August 11 the *Melrose Abbey* commenced loading at Immingham for Rafferty and Watson Ltd (freight £4,193 1s 10d) and set out for the Mediterranean where she discharged her cargo at Tarragona. On completion she proceeded to Casablanca where on September 9 she started to load phosphate for Sas van Gent (freight £2,237 17s 11d).

The *Neath Abbey* having completed unloading a cargo of iron ore at Middlesbrough in September, 1937 sailed in ballast for Sweden and on September 15 at 5pm having anchored at Hernosand was taken on time-charter by the Spanish Government at £4,750 per month. Initially the ship was employed carrying woodpulp from Utansjo and Bollsta to Valencia, then carrying a cargo of fruit from Almeria to Gothenburg and Stockholm, and then another cargo of woodpulp from Sweden to Barcelona and Valencia. It is interesting to note who made the payments for this time-charter. The first monthly payment made in advance was by the Moscow Narodny Bank, then the next three months by the Oficina Commercial Espana and thereafter by the Mid-Atlantic Shipping Co. Ltd., a company in the United Kingdom set up by the Republicans to organise shipments via ships under the British flag.

Having discharged a cargo of phosphate at Sas van Gent during September, 1937 the *Melrose Abbey* was sent in ballast to Finland where she loaded woodpulp at Rauma and Spjutsund (Kotka) at a freight of £6,850 for the Spanish Commercial Delegation and discharged it at Valencia. After this she proceeded to Sfax where on October 20 she commenced to load a cargo of phosphate for Nantes (freight £3,508 6s 3d). She then proceeded to Rotterdam where a cargo of generals was loaded for Howard Tenens Ltd (freight £5,225) which was discharged at Barcelona. The ship then went back to Antwerp in ballast where a cargo of pig iron was loaded to the account of Howard Tenens Ltd. (freight £5,700) for Sagunto. The ship then proceeded to Valencia where on January 14, 1938 she commenced loading fruit for T.A. Finzi, Layman and Co. Ltd. (freight £4,378 6s 8d). Having taken a part cargo she moved on to Gandia to complete her cargo and then sailed for London. Having unloaded she ballasted across to Rotterdam where a cargo of barytes was loaded (freight £747 16s 7d) for Garston, whence she moved around to Swansea in ballast to load coal on behalf of Cory's Trading Ltd (freight £4,754 6s. 3d.) for Barcelona.

During February, 1938 Frederick Jones and Company took delivery of the first of two new ships on order at the yard of William Gray and Co. Ltd., West Hartlepool, and her first voyage was as follows. (*Margam Abbey*).

This new ship was immediately sent to Sunderland where she loaded a cargo on behalf of Atkinson, Prickett Ltd. This consisted of 3,736 tons 9 cwt of coal at 25/- per ton, totalling £4,651 12s 6d and 15 tons 3cwt of generals at the same rate £18 19s 6d destined for Barcelona.

The fact that the Russians were no longer willing to send ships to Spain meant that the Republicans were anxious to obtain ships to bring cargoes from Odessa in the Black Sea on their behalf. Knowing that the *Neath Abbey* was in a Spanish port in January, 1938 they informed

An Intelligence Photograph of the steamer *Margam Abbey* taken off Ceuta.          *(Laurence Dunn collection)*

Frederick Jones and Company that they intended to send the ship in ballast to Odessa to load for the Mediterranean Coast of Spain. Frederick Jones was none too pleased with this, as he feared that they would use the ship to carry armaments. However, his insurance had been paid on the basis of 10/- per cent, and this only allowed for trading as far East in the Mediterranean as Malta. Frederick Jones did his best to wriggle out of letting the ship carry out the voyage, but finally had to relent when his crew expressed their willingness to sail her, and when the Spanish offered a one off payment of £2,500 over and above her monthly freight of £4,750. This was to cover the extra cost of insurance, additional war bonus and bunkers which the firm would have to buy in Russia. When bought in 1934 the *Neath Abbey* had cost £7,500 and during the Spanish voyages she had been insured for £10,000 at 10/- per cent, costing £50. However, Frederick Jones had to pay at the rate of £8 per cent to insure the ship for this voyage, making a total of £800 to her £10,000 valuation.

The ship sailed East to the Black Sea on January 31 where she fortunately took an age to load her cargo at Odessa (whilst there she was out of harms way). She was at this time commanded by a very experienced Abbey Line master, Captain Jones, who on emerging back out into the Mediterranean skirted the North African coast and slipped into Oran on March 11 to wait his best opportunity for a passage across to Spain. He waited for five days and on March 16 in darkness slipped across to the safety of Aguilas a Republican held port where he waited for a day before slipping up the coast again under the cover of darkness into Valencia where the ship took over two weeks to unload her cargo of generals.

Meanwhile the two newer Abbey ships, *Melrose Abbey* and *Margam Abbey* were en route for Barcelona where they had docked early in March. On the night of March 16 Mussolini had ordered his air force to bomb Barcelona, and during the next two days a total of eighteen attacks were made on the city and its port with a resulting heavy loss of life. Fortunately the two new Abbey ships were undamaged, but while the *Melrose Abbey* was covered by war risk insurance throughout, the *Margam Abbey* still on her maiden voyage was subjected to such considerable delay that her cover ran out whilst the ship was in port. The cost to obtain cover for his brand new ship in a port subject to enemy attack was almost impossible, but eventually he achieved it, but had to pay the sum of £2,735 12s 10d. The freight for this voyage had been £4,670 12s 0d added to which demurrage for eleven days three hours at £30 per day – £333 15s 0d was paid by the Mid Atlantic Shipping Co. Ltd. Thus the profit which should have been considerable was reduced to £202 0s 11d.

It was apparent that the employment of a new ship in the trade was totally uneconomic from that point onwards, and Frederick Jones immediately set about withdrawing the two ships, *Melrose Abbey* and *Margam Abbey*. The *Melrose Abbey* was sent to Casablanca in ballast where on March

The *"Melrose Abbey"* loading iron ore at Algiers in July, 1938.

30 she commenced to load phosphate for Sas van Gent (freight £1,467) and following discharge ballasted back to Cardiff, arriving on April 12. Having paid such a high price to re-insure the *Margam Abbey* he decided to get a last cargo out of Spain with the ship. Thus on March 20 she left Valencia and moving along the coast loaded fruit at Denia, Alicante and Carthagena for London River at a freight made up of 180,000 cu.ft. @ 30/- per 100 cu.ft., plus demurrage for 4 days 2 hours at London at £30 per day = £122 10s 0d. (Profit £767 12s 6d). This homeward cargo was for the account of J. A. Finzi, Layman & Co. Ltd. On completion of discharge at London she made her way in ballast to Cardiff where she arrived on April 16.

Frederick Jones and his sons were very glad to see their two new ships and their loyal crews safely home, and the *Neath Abbey* was redelivered to the firm at Marseilles on April 4 on completion of her eventful time-charter. She was then sent to Sfax to load phosphate for Nantes before returning to Cardiff on May 2. The *Neath Abbey* had received some damage to her funnel during an air attack and she and the *Melrose Abbey* each spent a month at Cardiff for repairs and overhaul.

The new *Margam Abbey* after her eventful voyage was still only two months old and did not require any attention. Therefore she was quickly loaded for an outward passage to the Mediterranean, but I hasten to add, not for Spain.

In June, 1938 the second of the two ships on order at West Hartlepool was completed, and was given the name of *Tintern Abbey*.

However, although he had paid for the ship, Frederick Jones decided to leave her moored at West Hartlepool. When in the Spring of 1938 he had withdrawn the two new ships *Melrose Abbey* and *Margam Abbey* from the Spanish Republican trade, this was because they were too modern to provide anything like a realistic return as the war risks insurance had become prohibitive. However, there were no such penalties to be incurred in trading the *Neath Abbey*, as she had only cost £7,500 in the first place, and had virtually paid for the new ship anyway. Therefore the *Neath Abbey* was

88

returned to the trade to Spain, where she proved so successful in running the blockade. Meanwhile the new *Tintern Abbey* was left at West Hartlepool, unregistered, almost like a car in a showroom. She could not start to erode her four year gap to her first survey as she had not yet been registered. She was paid for, and was not burning any holes in the founders pocket. The ship she was due to replace was earning in a month what the new ship would take a year to earn in the way of profits, and Frederick wisely decided to leave well alone as the Spanish trade would not last for ever.

Thus after spending a month at Cardiff for repairs the *Neath Abbey* sailed from the port on June 2, 1938 in ballast for Havre where she loaded general cargo on behalf of Howard Tenens Ltd. (freight £3,500) and set off for Valencia. The rate had dropped since her last voyage but the shippers Howard Tenens Ltd agreed to pay the war risks insurance which was back to 10/- per cent. The profit for this outward passage totalled £1,192 0s 1d. On June 28 having discharged at Valencia she quickly proceeded to Sfax where she loaded phosphate for Sas van Gent.

After this the *Neath Abbey* was employed on a Kara Sea voyage for twelve weeks, where she was joined by the *Margam Abbey*.

In October, 1938 the *Neath Abbey* was time-chartered to the Spanish Government or more precisely Messrs J. A. Finzi, Layman and Co. Ltd., the hire being 16/- on her deadweight, ie £3,200 per month. The ship sailed from Cardiff on October 8 for Antwerp where she loaded foodstuffs for Carthagena and Almeria and after discharge returned to Antwerp in ballast arriving on November 21. She was quickly loaded again and set out two days later. There is no record of the ports she discharged at in Spain on this occasion but on January 4, 1939 the ship was handed back to Frederick Jones and Company at Tunis.

The ship then carried a cargo of phosphate from Tunis to Granville and on completion was brought around to Cardiff where she arrived on February 9, 1939. Frederick Jones and his sons could see that the Civil War in Spain was all but over. The ship was quickly sold, and her replacement, the *Tintern Abbey* was now commissioned. The *Neath Abbey* had provided some of the firm's greatest profits with a single ship, and between the period from July 23, 1934 to February 9, 1939 her total freights were £109,555 16s 10d yielding a profit of £45,000.

Thus the Abbey Line withdrew from the Spanish trade about twelve weeks before the conflict ended, but it is worth noting that although the *Neath Abbey* had received some minor damage, not one of their ships had actually figured in a casualty report due to the hostilities. A magnificent record.

General Franco kept his promise not to allow ships that had traded with the Republic to enter Spanish ports, as in

Having been left at West Hartlepool for a year, in April, 1939 the new *Tintern Abbey* was commissioned.

*(Welsh Industrial & Maritime Museum)*

the early part of the Second World War the *Melrose Abbey* was refused entry to Valencia where she had been directed by the British Ministry of War Transport to lift a cargo. As a result the firm had to divert the *Tintern Abbey* to get this cargo. It was as well that she had been left at her moorings until the civil war had ended.

Loss of the *Margam Abbey* during the Second World War. The vessel is shown in the Thames Estuary on April 25, 1940 having struck a mine. With her back broken she sinks slowly by the head.

## Chapter 9

# REPUBLICAN TERRITORY DIVIDED

The fall of Castellon on June 15, 1938 gave the insurgents a base in between the Republican held territory, and eventually they pushed further to the North. The increase in air attacks was alarming to many of the British merchant ship masters, and as a result, even before the fall of Castellon seven of them had lodged a protest with the British Consul on June 10 concerning the air attacks on their vessels at Barcelona. This protest was forwarded to the Foreign Office in London. It was made by Captain Nesbitt of the steamer *Gothic*, Captain C. Lewis (*Stanburn*), Captain A. Still (*Hamsterley*), Captain Lamb (*Sea Glory*), Captain Jones of the Welsh owned *Alex*, Captain G. Davies (*Stanbrook*) and the master of Pope's *Kenfig Pool*. Two of these ships were real veterans of the war having survived from the blockade of Bilbao, over a year earlier.

However the attacks continued; on June 15 all the British ships moored at Barcelona were badly shaken by an air attack on the port. Another veteran of the blockade in the North, the Guardian Line's *Macgregor* received damage to her bridge in this attack, but was able to leave port without undergoing repairs.

On the morning of the following day a seaman named Edgar Marquet of the *Seabank Spray* (ex-*Seven Seas Spray*), that ship of Alfred Pope's which had actually broken the Bilbao blockade, was killed in a raid on Barcelona. He had left the ship when the alarm was sounded and was running for an air raid shelter when a bomb burst near him. He died in an ambulance on the way to the hospital. The ship was undamaged in this raid, but other British ships had suffered damage.

On June 21 the Westcliffe Steamship Company's *Thorpeness* was sunk at her moorings at Valencia, only eleven days after the loss of her consort *Thorpehaven* at Alicante. In fact this company had lost three of its ships in barely a month to insurgent bombing.

On the morning of June 22 the Cardiff steamer *Sunion* was lying one mile outside Valencia when she was struck by

Claude Angel's *"Sunion"* was bombed and sunk off Valencia on June 22, 1938. *(York Collection)*

On June 27, 1938 the British steamer *Farnham* was bombed and sunk at Alicante.
*(Laurence Dunn Collection)*

two incendiary bombs. In the attack one bomb fell forward and one amidships, wrecking the bridge and setting her on fire. The vessel sank, but before this her crew of 32 and a German Non-Intervention officer were taken off, uninjured. The ship had been in ballast at the time and due to dock at Valencia in order to pick up passengers.

Later that day the *African Trader* was intercepted on the high seas off the coast of Spain by an insurgent seaplane, which circled round her and wirelessed the master ordering him to proceed to the Nationalist held Palma, Majorca. As a result the ship sent out a distress message which was intercepted by HMS *Imogen*. The Naval vessel went to her aid, and the seaplane made off. Subsequently the *African Trader* arrived at Valencia having been escorted to the three mile limit by the *Imogen*.

When the Billmeir steamer *Stanwold* arrived at Gibraltar the master reported having had a blank shot fired at his ship by a Nationalist trawler whilst he was sailing down the Spanish coast, but he had declined to stop for the insurgent ship. It is interesting to note the list of repairs which the *Stanhall* required following her bombing in May. It was far more serious than had been expected, and only became fully apparent when she was dry docked at Baltimore. It consisted of renewing twelve plates, one off and six fair, frames, beams, brackets, bulkheads, stringers, and deck plating straighten and renew, seams caulk, tanks test, hold ceiling part renew, deck fittings repair, rudder recondition, propeller blades straighten, draw shaft, and repairs to electrical lighting, together with sundry lighting. This was the pride of Jack Billmeir's fleet and he was none too pleased.

On June 27 the British steamers *Laleham*, *Bramden* and *Stanwold* were damaged by flying shrapnel during an air raid at Alicante. During the attack the steamer *Farnham* was sunk by a direct hit.

On the same day the Cardiff managed tanker *Arlon* was set on fire while lying at Valencia. The ship received one direct hit which set her on fire, while another bomb fell between the ship and the quay, and a dozen bombs fell alongside the quay near to the vessel. During this attack a member of her crew, a Rumanian was killed, and another was injured. At the time she had been discharging a cargo of 7,000 tons of aviation spirit from St. Louis, Rhona, although all but 100 tons had been unloaded. Such was the danger that the burning ship was towed out of the port and eventually sank off Nazaret Beach, one mile South of Valencia. When interviewed by the press the second officer gave this account.

> Planes dropped forty bombs in a straight line along the wharf, fifteen of them falling on the wharfside, one hitting us flush and another falling between us and the dock. We were due to sail in half an hour's time, as the vessel had been discharging since Saturday (June 25) and had only 100 tons of cargo left.

On July 10 the Belgian non-intervention officer on board the *Yorkbrook* was injured by flying shrapnel during an air attack at Valencia. A number of ships were hit by shrapnel, but no damage was caused. One bomb actually fell between the steamers *African Trader* and *Yorkbrook*.

Stone and Rolfe's *"Glynwen"* was damaged during the conflict.                    *(York Collection)*

A number of ships were turning up during this period asking for surveys due to previously unreported bomb damage in Spanish ports. On July 18 the Stone & Rolfe steamer *Glynwen* arrived at Gibraltar reporting damage in Spanish ports through bombing both in April and June 1938. The vessel was described as generally strained, slight leakage in her hold, peaks and engine-room.

Following her bomb damage at Barcelona in June, on July 19 the *Macgregor* turned up at Rouen where she was surveyed, and the following reported: starboard lifeboat chocks destroyed, all wood decks found leaking, five port lights broken, one ventilator tube destroyed, sun deck over bridge leaking, wireless and dynamo out of order, deck water service pipes damaged, auxiliary piping on deck damaged, sanitary tank leaking and other sundry damage. It was not too unusual for a ship damaged by bombing, if she was still seaworthy, to make for a port out of the war zone to effect repairs.

Two of Billmeir's steamers were damaged on July 19 while lying at Valencia. The *Stanland* was set on fire by a bombing attack by five insurgent aircraft. The damage was actually caused by a bomb landing in 250 drums of gasoline which were on the quay having been unloaded from the vessel. The bridge was set on fire and part of the accommodation scorched quite badly. However, the fire was put out after about an hour and on completion of discharging the vessel she was able to proceed to Oran for temporary repairs. At the same time the *Stangate* which was across the harbour from the *Stanland* was slightly damaged by shrapnel, when a bomb fell between the ship and an air raid shelter. Her master, Captain Bibbings from Cardiff and the majority of the crew were fortunately ashore at the time. The ship arrived at Marseilles on July 26 for survey, but repairs were not necessary.

The Welsh ships *Dellwyn* and *Bramhill*, both under the control of Claude Angel of Cardiff, were unloading at Gandia on July 22 when the port was raided at 11am and fifty bombs fell 200 yards away from the ships, which fortunately were undamaged. However the *Dellwyn* was to be the target for virtually constant attacks by the insurgents over the next five days, whilst the *Bramhill* had left the port after the first attack. The *Dellwyn* was struck by bombs and machine-gunned on the 25th, 26th and 27th, and on the latter date within a few hundred yards of a British warship she was finally sunk by a direct hit on the vessel. At the time the crew were ashore, and there were no casualties. After the conflict was over this ship was refloated by the Nationalists, and on May 10, 1939 following repairs was placed in the Spanish merchant fleet as the *Castillo Montesa*.

The *Dellwyn* was bombed and sunk at Gandia on July 27, 1938. She is shown under her earlier name of *Madge Llewellyn*.

*(Laurence Dunn Collection)*

The *Stanleigh* was the next of Billmeir's ships to be damaged. On July 28 she was hit by a bomb whilst lying at Valencia. The raid was undertaken by six Savoia aircraft and fifteen buildings were hit as well as the port church. Two members of the *Stanleigh*'s crew were injured, neither seriously. The bomb fell on the poop, penetrated to the storeroom and started a fire, which the crew put out before any serious damage could be caused.

At 2am on July 28 the *Stanwold* arrived at Gibraltar en route from Carthagena to London with a cargo of oranges. She had to put into port to effect temporary repairs following her sustaining damage at Alicante. The repairs to her steering gear and bridge took several days and the ship finally left Gibraltar on August 1 at 6pm for London.

The steamer *Kellwyn* formerly 'Potato Jones' *Marie Llewellyn* was one of a number of ships damaged by an aircraft attack on Valencia on July 28. Two men were killed in the attack, the Danish Non-Intervention officer and the Chinese cook whilst the ship suffered a number of small holes above her waterline and smashed doors and furniture in the accommodation. The mate and three other seamen were also wounded in the attack. The ship was unloading a cargo of coffee and sugar at the time.

The *Stanleigh* was attacked a second time whilst lying at Valencia, when on August 5 during an air raid two bombs landed between the vessel's hull and an air raid shelter. Numerous holes were blasted in the bridge, the chartroom was wrecked and a splinter a yard long was hurled into the engine-room where, however, the damage was not serious.

Such was the level of air attacks on Republican held ports that air raid shelters had been erected in port areas. When an air raid commenced the stevedores, dock workers and ship's crews would quickly leave the ships and take refuge. Indeed some ships crews were actually housed ashore, where possible, away from the most dangerous areas, when cargo was not being discharged. This constant volume of air attacks created long delays and congestion in ports, and instead of ships being able to discharge their cargoes in days or up to a week, the time in port was extended in cases up to two or three weeks. This made the job of carrying cargo to and from the Republic even more dangerous. The majority of ships engaged in the trade were now operating what amounted to a feeder service from Marseilles and Oran, whilst ships not prepared to take such risks were discharging at those ports instead of running the gauntlet. One aspect of the crews leaving their ships when an air attack was imminent was that those casualties amongst the crews were often killed and injured on the quays whilst running for cover.

The British Government made repeated protests to General Franco about these air attacks, although it was clear that in addition to insurgent aircraft, German and Italian forces were also involved. In one reply General Franco published a list of vessels which, he claimed were British and had been carrying munitions for the Barcelona Government. It was claimed that since January 1, 1937 more than 200 ships flying the British flag had attempted to carry contraband to Barcelona Government ports. The same reply also mentioned the names of a number of companies which it claimed were engaged in the arms traffic to Spain. Franco stated:–

> Britain has an easy remedy to stop the bombing of her merchant ships, this is by prohibiting the use
> of the British flag to protect the undignified contraband traffic in arms in the Republican zone.

94

Nobody doubts the final outcome of the war. Why try to lengthen Republican resistance?

The majority of British ships were lawfully engaged in carrying cargoes of foodstuffs and other materials, and lifting fruit for export from the Republic and since the date quoted indeed about 200 British ships had been trading to the Republic, but they were not all, if any, engaged in carrying arms. The British Government, had given strict instructions that the Royal Navy were to keep a close eye on this aspect, and whilst no doubt a few took a chance, it was very isolated.

The Burgos or Nationalist Government went on to list British ships which it alleged were engaged on carrying munitions to the Republic.

*Orange* – Left Marseilles on April 30 for Barcelona with explosives. (No such ship listed in Lloyd's Register).

*Bramhill* – Left Marseilles on April 30 for Barcelona with shells and cartridges. (Ship owned by Bramhill Steamship Co. Ltd., managers Claude Angel and Co. Ltd. Ship registered at Newport, Monmouthshire).

*Fenja* – Left Marseilles on April 30 for Port Mahon, Minorca with munitions and provisions. (Swedish vessel).

*Isadora* – Left Marseilles on May 21 for Republican Spain with munitions. (Ship bombed and sunk on June 9 at Castellon).

*Kellwyn* – Left Marseilles on May 21 with munitions for Republican Spain, (Ship managed by Claude Angel, Cardiff).

*Muneric* – Left Odessa for Barcelona and passed through the Bosphorus on April 25. Despite an investigation at Palermo (Italy) it unloaded at Barcelona five planes, 935 light machine guns, 24 heavy machine guns, 149 lorries, and rolls of barbed wire. (Ship owned by Counties Ship Management Co. Ltd., London).

*Gripfast* – Left Amberes for Almeria with armoured plates and barbed wire. (Ship owned by the Newbigin Steam Shipping Co. Ltd., Newcastle).

*Dover Hill* – From Russia to Alicante, passed through the Bosphorus on April 20 with 200 lorries and 400 tons of war materials. (Ship owned by Dover Steamship Co. Ltd., and registered at Glasgow).

*Marklyn* – From Newcastle to Gibraltar, thence left for Republican zone May 5 with barbed wire and long cases. (British owned).

*Stanburgh* – Left Amberes for Valencia May 15 with cargo suspected to include 20 million cartridges. (Ship owned by the Stanhope Steamship Co. Ltd., London. Manager J. A. Billmeir).

*Latymer* – Flying the British flag, owned by a Greek and chartered by Republican agents, with other ships flying the Greek flag plying between Odessa, the Piraeus and Marseilles, passed the Bosphorus on May 15 with lorries and accessories, and picked up at Piraeus cartridges, shells and tanks for Valencia. (No such ship listed in Lloyd's Register).

*Dover Abbey* – Left Gibraltar for Alicante on June 3 with Russian tanks camouflaged as lorries, and munitions, all shipped at Le Havre. (Ship owned by Anglo-Iberian Co., London).

The statement also gave a list of British companies which it said were shipping materials to Republican Spain.

Stanhope Company, which owned only two ships before the Spanish war; and today owns nineteen. Billmeir Company, which organised the Stanhope Company, and formed five other companies for the same trade. These (it claimed) were the Westcliff Shipping Company, Thameside Shipping Company, Veronica Steamship Company, Dillwyn Steamship Company and Trent Maritime Company, all of which were formed after the Spanish war started. The name of the Mid-Atlantic Company was also given.

In relation to the shipping companies Franco had almost got it right, other than the fact that Billmeir did not have a financial interest in the latter five. He did however, act in most cases as cargo brokers for all of them. Clearly the allegations about specific ships were rather wild. The Admiralty would never have allowed a British ship to call at Gibraltar with munitions. They were actively inspecting a great number of British ships to ensure that any allegation, such as this one, were without foundation.

Reaction to the insurgent statement was swift. Claude Angel of Cardiff, who managed both the *Bramhill* and *Kellwyn* stated:–

The *"Stanlake"* joined the fleet of the Stanhope Steamship Co., Ltd. in 1938. She is shown under her earlier name of *"Ruckinge"*.
*(Welsh Industrial & Maritime Museum)*

The *Bramhill* and *Kellwyn* have been carrying coal and general cargo for the Barcelona Government. The *Bramhill*, I believe, is at Almeria. The *Kellwyn* is carrying a cargo of wheat.

I think that this statement is probably a true account of the ship's employment.

Another South Wales shipowner was quoted by the Daily Mail at the time as saying:–

General Franco is very well informed as to the nature of the cargoes leaving British ports for Spain. He has an agent in every port and he is watching the departure of all vessels. Ships engaged in carrying shells and ammunition are owned mainly by foreigners.

Mr. Edward R. Newbigin, the 75 year old Managing Director of the Newbigin Steam Shipping Company was quoted as saying "It's a wicked lie" in reply to Franco's allegations that the *Gripfast* was carrying armour plates and barbed wire to the Barcelona Government, Mr. Newbigin continued:–

This ship has never loaded any cargo in any French port for Spain. She has been to Spain a few times but never taken anything but coal, coke or foodstuffs on the outward journey, and she has generally brought back fruit.

Most of the cargo being carried to Republican Spain was consigned in British ships, of which a considerable number were owned and/or managed in South Wales. The Republicans were still receiving arms and indeed someone was carrying them. I leave the readers to form their own opinion.

Returning back to the war zone, the steamer *Lake Lugano* was bombed and sunk off Palamos. This ship reflected her owners Swiss origins, although he lived in London, and the vessel flew the British flag. This happened on August 6, 1938.

On August 11, at 11.30am the *Stanlake* was damaged during an air raid at Valencia, when she was raked with machine-gun bullets, and a number of bombs landed near her. There were no casualties among the crew, but the ship was holed in several places above the waterline, and her two lifeboats were damaged.

Four days later at Valencia Mr. R.A. Amery, the wireless operator of the *Hillfern* was killed on the quay during one of the four successive air raids on the port. On the same day the British Non-Intervention observer on the *Fredavore* was wounded when he was hit by shrapnel. Neither of the ships were damaged in the attacks.

On August 19 the *Stanlake* which had just left Barcelona for Oran was attacked by an aircraft when 15 miles off the coast. Fortunately the bombs missed, there was no damage, and the vessel continued on her voyage.

The legendary little *Stanbrook* was not to be so lucky that day. She was the subject of an air attack whilst lying at Vallcarca, to the South of Barcelona. In the first of two raids, a bomb landed on the bridge and another in No. 1 hold causing a hole in her hull. The ship started to sink slowly, but the crew's attempt to beach her failed. The ship was further damaged in a second raid, causing another hole below the waterline, adjacent to No. 2 hold. The ship settled by the head, listing heavily, until she had rested on the bottom. However, although her cargo of cement was ruined, the ship was refloated on August 23 and towed to Barcelona, where she was drydocked and successfully repaired. There had been no casualties amongst the ship's personnel.

A day later Alfred Popes *Seabank Spray* was attacked at sea off the Spanish coast by an Italian aircraft which dropped bombs near the vessel which fortunately missed. The ship made port without damage or casualties.

Barnetts ship *Lucky* was subjected to an air attack on September 1, whilst lying at Aguilas, but she only received minor damage. Although casualties ashore were heavy, no one was injured on board.

The *Seabank Spray* and the *Bobie* were at Barcelona on September 13 when two squadrons of insurgent aircraft attacked the city. Both ships received damage from shrapnel and concussion. Captain Johns of the *Bobie* and his Dutch chief engineer received cuts and bruises in the attacks, while two men on the quay were killed. The damage was not severe enough to prevent them from sailing when their cargo had been discharged.

During September, 1938 survey was carried out on the *Nailsea Lass* at Barry in respect of previously unreported damage which had been sustained by the vessel being bombed at Valencia on January 6 and subsequent dates, and at Carthagena on July 12. This ship which was managed by E.R. Management Co. Ltd., of Cardiff, was repaired at Barry and thereafter resumed trading, although I have no information as to whether she went back to Spain or not.

On September 16 a number of British ships were damaged during an air attack on Barcelona. The *Stanlake* was seriously damaged by a bomb which exploded on the poop, but holed her, fortunately above the waterline. The *Bobie* was slightly damaged by shrapnel, the Greek cook M. Athanasy being injured in the head. The *Seabank Spray* and *Lake Hallwil* which were both at anchor were slightly damaged in the attack.

The *African Mariner* and the American *Wisconsin* received some damage at Barcelona on September 24 when a bomb exploded in the water fifty yards from their sterns. In the same attack the Billmeir steamer *Stanholme* was quite badly damaged. Her midships section and the stern were badly smashed, and her mainmast had gone over the side due to the amount of damage caused by the attack.

On October 3 the *African Mariner* still at Barcelona, was not so lucky. As a direct hit was recorded on the vessel. The bomb ploughed its way through two decks and exploded in her cargo of wheat blowing out the bulkhead. There were no casualties. Her master was Captain P.H. Manley of Penarth. Apparently the cargo of wheat had cushioned the impact of the explosion as the ship was not that seriously damaged.

On the following day a number of British ships were damaged in an air attack on the port, including the *Gothic, Thorpebay, Lake Hallwill* and Claude Angel's *Hillfern*. Nobody was injured, and the ships were only superficially damaged.

On October 9 the steamer *Bramhill* was lying at Barcelona when she was hit by a bomb and set on fire when an insurgent seaplane raided the port at about 10pm. The bomb tore an 8ft. hole in the vessel's deck amidships. This direct hit damaged the cabin of the mate and the second officer. Fragments of the bomb were scattered over a large area of the vessel, while two other bombs, one of which fell on the quay and the other in the sea, also caused damage in the form of small holes in the hull above the waterline. It was thought that the bomb might have sunk the ship had not the explosion spent all its main force in the coal bunker. The master, Captain Thomas Parker and the crew were ashore at the time of the bombing. The explosion caused steampipes to burst and consequently put the winches out of commission for a while, resulting in delays, in the discharging of her cargo, which consisted of beans and beef.

At Valencia on October 10 the steamer *Transit* managed by David Barnett of Cardiff was hit by a bomb during one of three insurgent air attacks on the port during the night. The ship was unloading a cargo of coal from Oran at the time and was extensively damaged. The deck and superstructure were badly holed and buckled but fortunately there was no damage below the waterline, and no danger of the vessel sinking. Owing to an early alarm the crew had gone ashore to refuges before the bomb fell. This ship was actually Lord Glanely's old *Molton* which had been captured by the Nationalist cruiser *Almirante Cervera* on July 14, 1937 off Santander and released on September 10 of that year. She had been sold to the Continental Transit Co. Ltd., of London in 1938 and placed under the management of David P. Barnett of Cardiff under the name *Transit*.

Three days later the *Stancroft* was severely damaged when a bomb scored a direct hit on the vessel at Barcelona.

The bomb landed on her after deck and part of the deck was destroyed and a fire started which took half an hour to extinguish. The ship sprang a leak, and her master, Captain Leonard Spence, of Redcar, Yorkshire, instructed his crew to take their belongings ashore before she settled on the bottom. During the same attack the *Stanholme* was further damaged, having all her doors and part of the bridge blown away. She was not however, in a sinking condition.

The Barnett managed steamer *African Explorer* and another British steamer, the *Lake Hallwil* were badly damaged during a heavy raid on Barcelona on the morning of October 19. The ship received a direct hit when a bomb passed through her deck, exploded in her cargo of wheat and made a large hole in her side above the waterline. Three of her crew, all foreign, were wounded as a result. Subsequently the ship completed the discharge of her cargo and made for a port outside the war zone for survey and temporary repairs.

Valencia suffered a heavy insurgent attack on the evening of November 1, when three waves of bombers flew over the city at 7pm, 9pm and 11.20pm. During the attack the steamer *Stangate* was struck by bomb fragments but the extent of the damage was not severe.

General Franco's forces were getting more daring. He sent an armed merchant vessel, the *Nadir* into the North Sea in order to intercept Republican merchantmen which were trading outside the war zone. It came as a shock to the world to hear that on November 2, 1938 the *Nadir* had intercepted and shelled a Spanish merchant ship, the *Cantabria* off Great Yarmouth. Although this incident was outside British territorial waters it was virtually in sight of Great Yarmouth itself. The ship shelled the *Cantabria* for about two hours commencing at 2pm. Of the 37 onboard the merchantman, including three women and five children, the majority were taken on board the *Nadir* and the steamer *Pattersonian*. However, the *Cantabria's* master, Captain Manuel Arguelles, his wife, two children and the second steward were rescued by the Cromer lifeboat.

The British Government were most concerned by this event which was extending the conflict, now to the shores of the United Kingdom itself.

When the civil war broke out, there were many difficulties experienced by those serving on Spanish merchant ships. The owners of these ships were domiciled in both zones of Spanish territory, and the crews were often of different political persuasions, this resulted in ships not wanting to return to one or other of the different zones, (a) because the owner lived in another, and (b) because the crew or part of the crew were of another zone. In some cases crews actually refused to sail the ships and in others the owners refused to allow them to proceed to one or other of the zones. Many Spanish ships were moored in different parts of the world, some staying in port throughout the conflict. Others continued sailing, but staying away from Spain itself, and finding employment in the general tramp trades. In cases of ships being under Nationalist control, the Republican Government took action through the courts to seize the various vessels and take over the control of their movements. In effect they were quite lawfully able to nationalise any Spanish ship not controlled in Republican held territory. Many Spanish ships tried in the early days to make it to their home ports in Spain, usually Republican held with cargoes, and these were often attacked in International Waters by Nationalist warships and captured or sunk. There were cases recorded of Spanish merchantmen being chased into French waters and shelled and sunk, to the horror and displeasure of the French Government, in their own territorial waters. Protests were made and threats made to the insurgent forces.

The result of these attacks and the clear dangers in which Spanish Merchant ships found themselves was to see fewer and fewer of them putting to sea. A considerable number were laid up in the United Kingdom. This was one of the major reasons why such a large proportion of the cargoes taken to and from Republican held Spanish ports were carried in British ships.

On November 3 the *Stanburn* was hit whilst lying at Valencia. A bomb fell in No. 1 hold and made a hole in her hull below the waterline. The vessel in leaking condition was pumped out and temporary repairs effected. The Chief Engineer was slightly injured, and her precious cargo off foodstuffs was removed before it could be spoiled. The vessel was, after repairs able to proceed.

The *Stanburgh* was not so fortunate, as on November 4 whilst lying at the French port of Etang de Thau, Sete, she was ripped apart by an explosion whilst loading petrol destined for Spain. So severe was the damage that the vessel had to be abandoned, and subsequently sold for breaking up where she lay.

Our old friend *Yorkbrook* was the victim of yet another attack, when on November 6 she was damaged by an air attack whilst lying at Almeria in ballast. No casualties were incurred on the ship, but a number of rivets were started, although this was only of a minor nature. She subsequently made for Oran for survey and repairs, and then loaded for Valencia.

Reginald Jones' *Candleston Castle* was the subject of an air attack at Barcelona on November 12 during which little

Claude Angel's *"Kaolack"* was bombed and damaged at Valencia on November 25, 1938.

Below: David Barnett's steamer *"Cemenco"* was also bombed and damaged at Valencia on November 25, 1938.

*(John Clarkson)*

damage was caused by the flying shrapnel, but two members of crew were injured. Mr. N.W. James, the third engineer received a broken leg whilst fireman Ali Ahmed was slightly injured. Both were put ashore into hospital and the ship eventually left port without them.

At about this time the *African Explorer* whilst at Carthagena received further damage which necessitated her proceeding to Marseilles where repairs were carried out.

The *Stanwold* was at this time operating a feeder service from Oran to Valencia. On November 14 she was slightly damaged during an air attack at Valencia, but arrived back at Oran three days later. Eight days later the *Stanwold* back in Valencia again was badly damaged in an attack which also damaged three other British merchantmen, the *Bobie*, *Kaolack* and *Cemenco*. The *Stanwold* after effecting temporary repairs was able to leave, and on November 28 headed for Marseilles for a more thorough examination.

On November 23 Alfred Popes *Kenfig Pool* was one of three ships slightly damaged during an air attack at

Barcelona. On that same day our old friend Claude Angel's *Bramhill* was slightly damaged at Barcelona, but in all these cases no casualties were suffered amongst the crews.

On November 28 two Billmeir ships were damaged by air attack at Barcelona. These were the *Stanwell* and *Stangrove*. A bomb hit the deck of the *Stanwell* squarely, penetrating below, where it exploded, badly perforating the vessels side. The explosion wrecked the forecastle quarters, starting a small fire which was quickly extinguished. The deck equipment, winches and forward mast were damaged and the steam connections severed, but temporary repairs were subsequently made. Two other bombs narrowly missed the vessel, one falling in the water astern and the other on the quay. The *Stanwell* was unloading a cargo of coal. The *Stangrove* was slightly damaged by fragments when a bomb hit the quay alongside her.

The steamer *Stanhall* had for some time, being Jack Billmeir's pride and joy, been kept out of the Spanish war zone since the damage caused to her during an air raid some time earlier. It was now something of a surprise to see that Billmeir was involved in carrying cargo for another conflict. He was not a man to miss opportunities. On November 26 it was reported that the *Stanhill* was unloading a cargo of 6,000 tons of arms and ammunition for China. At this time a conflict was ensuing between the Chinese and Japanese, and indeed the Japanese were fighting and taking Chinese territory. The cargo of arms had been carried on the *Stanhill* from Russia, and part of the cargo was sent by rail to Lashio, a Burmese town, 18 miles from the Chinese frontier, and thence by road to China, while the rest, consisting of explosive, was shipped up the Irrawaddy by boat to Bhamo, 40 miles from the border and thence by road.

The Chinese were having trouble getting supplies through to their troops and clearly Jack Billmeir was their man. In this instance there was absolutely no pretence as to the nature of the cargo. There was no law in the United Kingdom to prohibit the carriage of arms for the Chinese, and Billmeir did his best to satisfy their requirements. A number of his ships were to be involved in the trade, but these tended to be his more modern and larger vessels, where the risks of interception by the Japanese Navy, although very real, was less risky than those in the Spanish conflict.

Returning to the Spanish Civil War, the number of attacks on Republican held ports by insurgent aircraft had increased considerably. In line with this activity, the instances of damage to Jack Billmeir's ships had also increased. On December 1 the crew's quarters of the *Stanwell* were damaged by a bomb whilst the vessel was lying at Barcelona. Two days later the *Stanland* also at Barcelona was holed below the waterline and had her crew quarters destroyed by a bomb during an air raid. Fortunately none of the crew were injured, as they were now spending more time ashore, either being housed ashore or taking refuge in air raid shelters.

On December 5 at Barcelona the *Stanwell* was badly damaged on the starboard side by a bomb. She was one of three ships hit during an air raid, the others being the *Transit* and *Noemijulia*. In a further raid later that day the *Stanwell* was again hit, as was her consort *Stanhope* and the *Transit* and *African Mariner*. The valiant *Stanwell* whilst still at Barcelona was to survive further attacks on December 6 and 10, which increased the amount of damage suffered by the vessel. It was a wonder that some of these Billmeir owned ships could still float.

On December 14 the *Stanholme* was entering the port of Valencia with a cargo of coal when she was hit by shrapnel during an air attack.

The Nationalist forces were intensifying their bombardment of the Catalan Province, and it is truly amazing how the same ships were being damaged time and again. It is clear that many of these ships were running a very risky and efficient feeder service to the Republican ports from Oran and Marseilles, and that their cargoes of mostly foodstuffs were badly needed by the civilian populations barely existing on what must by now have been a starvation diet. No one would pretend that the shipowners were motivated by any ideological ideals, but having been involved in many cases with supplying the Republican side from the start of the conflict, albeit for handsome returns, it is surely to their credit that they didn't desert them now when the going was getting rough. It was definitely getting very dangerous in the South and South East of Spain.

Having been severely damaged on October 13 at Barcelona the *Stancroft* had been successfully raised and was in the process of being repaired when a further blow befell the vessel. As on December 27 she was again bombed at Barcelona, and once again the ship sank at her moorings. Unfortunately Barcelona was under siege by now and was under almost constant air attack. As a result there was no way that Billmeir could get her raised and repaired and she had to be abandoned. On April 19, 1939, some three months after the Nationalists took Barcelona she was successfully raised and subsequently repaired by them. Thereafter she was renamed *Castillo Almansa*, placed under the Spanish flag and traded as such for many years.

Knowing how Franco and his forces felt about Jack Billmeir and his valiant fleet of ships it was no surprise that Billmeir never saw his ship again. It is quite clear that Billmeir was a thorn in the side to the Nationalists, and without his intervention and support the Republicans would not have survived thus far. Franco knew this.

Another Barnett managed vessel was the victim of an insurgent air raid on December 28 at Valencia. This was the *Emerald Wings* which was struck by a bomb which caused considerable damage. Three of the crew were injured in this attack. Back in Barcelona, the *Transit* was one of three ships slightly damaged when shrapnel from bombs landing on the quay hit them on January 4, 1939. Ten days later the *Bellwyn* was struck by shrapnel during an air raid on Valencia, but she was little damaged. Also on January 14 the *Stanwell* was again damaged by an air attack while lying at Barcelona. She received serious damage to her superstructure and accommodation, and both sides of the vessel's hull were riddled above the waterline. A fire started but the flames were quickly put out by the crew and the local fire service. On the same day the *Stanforth* received damage to her bridge house and her hull during an air raid at Carthagena. But she proceeded to Gibraltar for survey of the damage and temporary repairs.

On January 22 the port of Valencia was again under insurgent air attack, five Savoia bombers being involved which dropped about fifty bombs. On this occasion the Billmeir steamer *Stanholme* was hit by shrapnel which badly damaged the plating on the port side of her stern.

The damaged *Stanwell* managed to leave Barcelona a few days before the fall of Barcelona, and made it to Marseilles where repairs were immediately put in hand.

The last Billmeir ship to leave Barcelona before it fell was the *Stancroft*. She had only managed to cover seven miles when she was subjected to three air attacks in the space of an hour. In the first she was attacked by seven aircraft and as a result the vessel turned back. However after a short space of time she resumed her voyage to be attacked by five aircraft and again by a further three. The Nationalist air force couldn't have been that good because they did not score a single hit and the ship, undamaged was subsequently escorted into Port Vendres by an Admiralty tug.

Nationalist forces had taken Tarragona on January 15, 1939, and were finally to capture Barcelona on January 26, and thereafter resistance on the Catalan Province was soon crushed. However, before the fall of Barcelona some of the veterans of the Spanish Civil War were to be found, as in the Bilbao and Santander campaign, hanging on to the very last minute still supplying the port. The last weeks in Barcelona were to be extremely costly to British shipowners.

The *Seabank Spray* was at Barcelona on January 21 when she received a direct hit on her cargo of coal, but was only slightly damaged. The *African Mariner* was damaged amidships during a raid the following day. This ship was unloading a valuable cargo of wheat and frozen meat. On January 22 the old stalwart of the civil war *Yorkbrook* was hit and sunk by a bomb which exploded and holed her below the waterline. The *African Mariner* was again struck by bombs on this day and as a result four Greek members of crew killed. Such was the damage that she sank in the port on the 23rd. The steamers *Huntress* and *Dover Abbey* were also badly damaged in this period. The former ship had received fourteen holes in her hull forward but fortunately they were all above the waterline.

Further attacks on Barcelona on January 24 and 25 resulted in even further damage to vessels in the port, including bombs hitting the *Dover Abbey, Thorpebay*, the French *Yolande* which sank as a result, the *Huntress* and *Seabank Spray*, and Claude Angel's tanker *Miocene* which also sank.

Barcelona fell to the Nationalist forces on January 26 and just before the city fell, in fact the day before, the surviving British ships although badly damaged left the port for Marseilles. It was obvious that Barcelona was doomed, but surprising that the ships had left it so late to make good their escape, as the last days at Barcelona had seen four ships lost in the port due to insurgent bombing. It was a bedraggled quartet of ships which docked at Marseilles, these were the London registered *Thorpebay*, the Gibraltar registered *Bobie* which was controlled by Alfred Pope, the legendary *Seabank Spray* which once again had been chancing her luck and the Barnett ship *Huntress*.

Thus with the fall of Barcelona another chapter of the civil war came to an end.

## Chapter 10
# THE FINAL MONTHS OF THE CONFLICT

After the steamer *Seven Seas Spray* had reached Bilbao on April 20, 1937 the owner Alfred Pope had said, "General Franco is not going to keep a single one of our ships from going about its lawful occasions". He had carried out the promise as the same ship, albeit now called *Seabank Spray* together with his chartered vessel *Bobie* and the other two ships only left Barcelona within hours of the insurgents taking the city. However, even Alfred Pope could see that the conflict was drawing to a close, and thereafter withdrew his damaged ships from the trade.

The remaining Republican territory now bordered Madrid in the West, Valencia in the North and Almeria to the South, and included Carthagena and Alicante.

Barnett's steamer *Emerald Wings* was damaged by an air attack at Carthagena on February 5 when five warplanes dropped fifty bombs on the town. This attack resulted in two members of the ship's crew being killed, the cook John Philips and an Arab fireman. On February 9 Barnett's other ship, *Atlantic Guide* was damaged by bomb splinters at Valencia, but no casualties were reported amongst her crew.

Meanwhile on February 5 the little *Stangrove* was making her way along the Spanish coast outside territorial waters with a cargo of mercury, sulphur, nitrate potash and nitrate ammonia en route from Valencia to Port Selva, when she was bombed and machine-gunned by insurgent aircraft. As a result her master, Captain Richards of Whitchurch, Cardiff, gave instructions to the crew to abandon ship and take to the lifeboat, remaining himself on board. The aircraft then disappeared and the master ordered the lifeboat's return. Owing to the rough sea then running the lifeboat was wrecked. The following day an insurgent destroyer hove in sight and, after firing warning shots at the *Stangrove*, ordered her to stop. A guard of eleven armed men was then sent on board the vessel and she was taken into Barcelona, which was now in insurgent hands, where a number of the crew were taken into custody. Later the vessel was ordered to proceed to Palma, Majorca, to which port she sailed under an armed escort. Whilst lying at this port the ship was

The steamer *"Atlantic Guide"* was bombed and damaged at Valencia on February 9, 1939.

(*Laurence Dunn*)

wrecked during a gale on February 23. However the Spanish salved her in 1941 and placed her into their fleet as the *Castillo del Oro*, and she survived thereafter until 1971 when she was delivered to shipbreakers in Spain.

Whilst Majorca and Ibiza had fallen to the Nationalists on July 19, 1936, the smaller Minorca had remained strongly Republican. On February 9, 1939 the hand over of Minorca was negotiated and took place under the supervision of the Royal Navy, who evacuated the Republican troops by agreement just prior to the Nationalist occupation taking place.

During an air raid on Valencia on February 9 the *Stanbrook* and *Stanforth*, which were in the process of unloading foodstuffs, were damaged by shrapnel. Ten days later while lying at Almeria the *Stanburn* was hit by shrapnel during another air attack by insurgents.

The *Emerald Wings* was damaged during an air attack, when Carthagena was bombed on February 10, but no casualties were reported and little damage sustained. On that same day another of David Barnett's fleet, the *Lucky* was hit during an air raid at Valencia when a bomb exploded in her No. 1 hold.

However, the ship did not live up to her name and quickly sank by the head, although fortunately there were no casualties on board. The steamer *Transeas* was also slightly damaged when an attack occurred on Valencia on February 26.

On March 8, 1939 the Nationalist Forces announced a blockade of all the Mediterranean coast Spanish ports:–

> The whole of the Mediterranean coast of Spain between Adra and Sagunto is closed for navigation to all kinds of ships of whatever nationality and whatever kind of cargo; no ships should approach it without the proper authorisation of the Admiral in Chief of the blockade force of the Mediterranean within a distance of three miles. Any ship not observing these instructions will be seized. Navigators are warned that off the fortified base of Carthagena and along the stretch of coast between the Torre de Mesa Light and Cabo Palos there will be submarines with orders to sink any ship which attempts to approach the coast within the three mile limit, no matter what the nationality of the ship may be. Ships proceeding with cargo for other ports on the coast in the 'red' zone, whatever their nationality, should go to ports in liberated Spain, preferably Barcelona, Palma, (Majorca), or Malaga.

The steamer *"Transeas"* was damaged by bombing in February and March, 1939. She is shown under the earlier name of *"Polmela"*.

(R.M. Parsons)

The Dillwyn Steamship Company's "Bellwyn" refused to submit to a Nationalist warship off Southern Spain on March 10th, 1939.

This in effect declared another blockade, but this time the war was all but over. However, there were still a few British ships left in the zone at this time.

At 9.32pm on March 10, the Welsh steamer *Bellwyn* gave out the following distress call.

> *Bellwyn*, position Cape San Antonio bearing 170 degrees; 23 miles distant; ordered to Palma, Majorca, by warship. Immediate assistance. Steamer *Stangate* under escort, proceeding Palma, Majorca. (remainder jammed).

At 10.24pm the following message was sent by the *Bellwyn,* addressed to all British warships.

> Refused to submit, now left alone. Please rescue steamer *Stangate* being taken to Palma, Majorca.

Apparently the *Stangate* was en route from Valencia to Almeria to load a cargo of oranges destined for London, and was in company with the *Bellwyn* when they were both ordered to stop by a Nationalist warship. Both ships tried to make for the coast and evade capture, but the *Bellwyn* was more fortunate, as the warship, predictably, concentrated her attentions more on the Billmeir ship. The *Bellwyn* had refused to submit, but the *Stangate* was captured by the insurgent ship. As a result of the *Bellwyn's* distress message the Royal Navy sent the destroyers HMS *Intrepid* and HMS *Impulsive* to investigate. They found the *Stangate* making for Majorca under escort of the insurgent warship, and immediately demanded her release, which they achieved without any incident or problems. The ship was then escorted to Gibraltar.

Due to the intensity of the Nationalist blockade, when the *Stancor* left Valencia on the night of March 14 with 200 refugees on board she was escorted by the cruiser HMS *Devonshire* to ensure that the British merchantman was not interfered with.

On March 16 the Billmeir ship *Stanhope* left Gandia for Gibraltar, and having made it out into International waters (outside the three mile limit) she was intercepted by a Nationalist warship which directed her towards Palma, and commenced to escort her. The merchant ship's radio operator only managed to get off a short distress call, "British steamer *Stanhope* in distress" before her radio was jammed. However, the Royal Navy sent HMS *Sussex* to investigate, and when found she secured the release of the Billmeir ship. Thereafter, when the Spanish ship was out of sight the *Stanhope* was instructed to proceed on her way, unescorted. There were no further incidents on the ship's passage to Gibraltar.

Having been released by the Royal Navy on March 10, the *Stangate* ever cheeky, was again stopped off the Spanish coast by an insurgent warship which placed an armed guard on board, and then escorted her to Palma. On this occasion

104

Dating from 1904 the *"Stancor"* was bought by Jack Billmeir in 1936. She is shown during 1937 whilst flying the Latvian flag for a short period.

*(John Clarkson)*

she was not so lucky, as the Royal Navy were unable to locate her to intervene. However, after the fall of the Republic the vessel was released and allowed to proceed from the region.

On March 29 Valencia fell to the Nationalists, and Madrid was also taken when the defending forces withdrew from their positions. On that same day the Cardiff managed steamer *Atlantic Guide* was approaching Valencia, blissfully unaware of the situation, and was subjected to machine-gunfire from an aircraft. At the time she was negotiating to take on board refugees which she did in fact succeed in doing.

On March 30 the last ships to leave Spain, the *African Trader* with a thousand or so refugees, and the Billmeir ship *Stanbrook* with 1,800 departed from Alicante. The last stronghold of Republican resistance, Almeria, Carthagena and Alicante fell to Franco's forces on March 31, and the civil war was officially ended on April 1, 1939.

It was fitting that the last British merchantmen to give service to the Republic had been one owned by Jack Albert Billmeir.

# Chapter 11
# CONCLUSION

Of the ships engaged in the trade to Republican Spain twenty-seven ships flying the British flag were sunk, of which nine were owned and/or managed in South Wales. In addition many ships of a wide range of nationalities were captured or sunk. Of these the following were placed under the Spanish flag, including those that had been raised and repaired.

| Vessel | Nationality | New Name |
|---|---|---|
| African Mariner | British | Castillo Montjuich |
| Aunis | French | Castillo Validemosa |
| Azelma | French | Castillo Javier |
| Dellwyn | British | Castillo Montesa |
| Eleni | British | Castillo Vera |
| Ellinico Vouno | Greek | Castillo Mombeltran |
| English Tanker | British | Castillo Almenara |
| Everards | Latvian | Castillo Fuensaldana |
| Farnham | British | Castillo Montiel |
| Foynes | Irish | Castillo Riaza |
| Francois | French | Castillo Andrade |
| Gardelaki | Greek | Castillo Tarifa |
| Gaulois | French | Castillo Turegano |
| Greatend | British | Castillo Norena |
| Hordena | Panamanian | Castillo la Mota |
| Isadora | British | Castillo Frias |
| Jan | Danish | Castillo Coca |
| Janu | Panamanian | Castillo Arevalo |
| Juss | Estonian | Castillo Gibralfaro |
| Katayama | Russian | Castillo Ampudia |
| La Corse | French | Castillo Jarandilla |
| Lena | Greek | Castillo Moncada |
| Lensovet | Russian | Castillo Bellver |
| Liberte | French | Castillo Almodovar |
| Lucky | British | Castillo Benisano |
| Max Loels | Russian | Castillo Montealegre |
| Miocene | British | Castillo Pedraza |
| Nagos | Greek | Castillo Monforte |
| Nicolau Eleni | Greek | Castillo Madrigal |
| Pomaron | Estonian | Castillo Butron |
| Postishev | Russian | Castillo Olite |
| Reina | Panamanian | Castillo Olmedo |
| Skulda | Norwegian | Castillo Daroca |
| Skvortzov Stepanov | Russian | Castillo Maqueda |
| Smidovich | Russian | Castillo Penafiel |
| Stancroft | British | Castillo Almansa |
| Stangrove | British | Castillo del Oro |
| Sydney | French | Castillo Simancas |

| | | |
|---|---|---|
| *Thorpehaven* | British | *Castillo Guadalest* |
| *Tsyurupa* | Russian | *Castillo Villafranca* |
| *Victoria* | Greek | *Castillo Oropesa* |
| *Wintonia* | Panamanian | *Castillo Rioseco* |
| *Yorkbrook* | British | *Castillo Monteagudo* |

* Details of the Spanish names of vessels taken from La Marina Mercante y el Trafic Maritimo en la Guerra Civil by R.G. Echegaray (Libreria Editorial San Martin).

Whilst the blockade of Northern Spain was undertaken by the insurgents and a number of actions took place in which the Royal Navy had to intervene, there was a measure of understanding between the respective naval forces as to each other's positions. The greatest loss of life occurred due to insurgent air attacks, which were heavily supported by German and Italian forces.

The conflict had lasted for a total of 33 months and the participation of British merchant ships had clearly helped to stiffen Republican resistance. Without the supplies carried by these ships the civil war would have ended far earlier; Franco was well aware of this, and frequently complained about it.

Most of the British merchant ships which survived this conflict were to be lost in the Second World War which commenced five months later. Alfred Pope sold his ships and withdrew from shipowning altogether. His famous *Seven Seas Spray* was sold to become the *Jeanne M*, and as such while on a voyage from Cardiff to Lisbon fell victim to a torpedo from the German submarine *U37* on December 2, 1940.

And what of the legendary 'Potato' Jones who had rounded Cape Horn in sail at fourteen years of age, and brought an element of humour to that savage conflict called Spain? In the Second World War he injured his shoulder in a bombing attack on his ship, but within two months was ferrying troops from the beaches of Dunkirk. He died at home in his native Swansea in 1965 at 92 years of age.

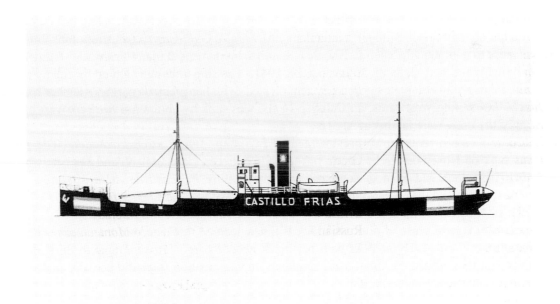

Drawing by Laurence Dunn of the *Isadora* after she had been raised and repaired after the conflict, and placed in the Spanish fleet as the *Castillo Frias*.

# ADDENDUM

In the early Summer of 1941, beleaguered Malta was calling for urgently needed food and war supplies and the enemy was making it impossible for merchant ships to get through even in escorted convoys. Remembering Jack Billmeir's record during the Spanish Civil War, the Admiralty approached him, and asked him to use his experience to try and get supply ships through to Malta. Billmeir agreed to make the attempt, and chose the steamer *Parracombe* to make the initial venture. The ship, heavily loaded with foodstuffs and all manner of war supplies, including Hurricane Fighters, left Methil and sailed coastwise to Oban where she joined a Southbound convoy. When off Gibraltar the ship was detached from the convoy and escorted to a point near the Straits where she was left to make the attempt to get through to Malta, alone. With one of Billmeir's most experienced masters aboard and a Spanish master to act as Pilot, the ship was quickly disguised as a Spanish merchantman and took a course which skirted the North African coast. An Italian aircraft flew over the ship, and the master feeling that the pilot had been satisfied by the disguise, felt more confident. However on May 6 the ruse had been seen through by the Italian forces and the ship was bombed and sunk with the tragic loss of thirty of her brave crew. The survivors were picked up by a French (Vichy) seaplane and landed in French North Africa where they were to spend many months incarcerated in very poor conditions. Eventually they were released, together with the crews of other unsuccessful ships making the attempt later under Billmeir's directions, and were repatriated. On arrival in Britain, Jack Billmeir, realising that they had suffered a terrible ordeal, paid out of his own pocket for each man to be fitted out with a new suit of clothes. A small, but well received token of his appreciation for what the men had been through.

Billmeir continued trying to get supplies through to Malta. For this purpose he had allocated five managed vessels. Unfortunately there was to be a heavy loss of life, but he did succeed in getting two ships through to Malta. Thereafter the supplies were taken in heavily armed escorted convoys under Admiralty supervision using fast cargo liners. Of the ships which made the attempt under Billmeir's directions, the *Empire Guillemot* (5,641 gross tons, built 1919) * used every form of disguise to confound the enemy. She flew Spanish, French and Italian flags while sailing along the North African coast and finally reached Malta on September 19, 1941. The ship although sighted by enemy aircraft on more than one occasion, managed to complete her journey unmolested, with her precious cargo. Alas her luck ran out, after leaving Malta in ballast sailing Westwards, on October 24 she was sunk by an aircraft torpedo West of Galeta Island, and the survivors of her crew were landed at Algiers.

The Italians, now aware of Billmeir's ruse intercepted two ships flying foreign colours. The *Empire Pelican* (6,463/1919) was sunk on November 14 by an aircraft torpedo between Galeta Island and Tunisia; whilst the *Empire Defender* (5,649/1910) which had been in company with the *Empire Pelican* was sunk in similar fashion on the following day. The final loss whilst undertaking this hazardous voyage was the *Empire Barracuda* (4,296/1918) which was torpedoed and sunk by the German submarine *U77* before she reached the Mediterranean.

However it was with a great sense of pride that Jack Billmeir learned that a second managed steamer *Empire Gull* (6,408/1919) had reached Malta early in 1942 with her much needed cargo. It was tragic to think that so many had died in the attempt, but their efforts had not been completely in vain, as two ships did actually make it, and they too had made the attempt completely unescorted.

* *Malta: Blitzed But Not Beaten* by Philip Vella (Progress Press, Valletta for The National War Museum Association. (1985).

# P.M. HEATON PUBLISHING

Paul Heaton was born at New Inn, Pontypool, in 1944 and was educated at Greenlawn Junior School in New Inn and the Wern Secondary School at Sebastopol. At fifteen he commenced employment, at first in a local store and then with a builder's merchant. A year later he was appointed as a Deck Cadet in the Merchant Navy, with the Lamport & Holt Line of Liverpool, and served in their vessels *Chatham, Constable* and *Romney* usually in the Brazil and River Plate trades. He joined the Monmouthshire Constabulary (now Gwent) in 1963, and served at Abergavenny, Cwmbran, Newport, the Traffic Department, the Motor Cycle Section, as the Press Liaison Officer, and for five years represented Inspectors for the whole of Wales nationally on the Joint Central Committee of the Police Federation. He was promoted to sergeant in 1974 and Inspector in 1982. On his retirement he served as Market Inspector with the RSPCA for eight years and at the same time was Landlord of a Public House for three years. He has always maintained an interest in maritime history and in transport generally, and has had the following books published:–

*Reardon Smith 1905-1980* (1980)
*The Baron Glanely of St. Fagans and W.J. Tatem Ltd.,* with H.S. Appleyard (1980)
*The 'Redbrook', A Deep-Sea Tramp* (1981) four editions
*The 'Usk' Ships* (1982) two editions
*The Abbey Line* (1983)
*Kaye, Son & Co. Ltd.,* with K. O'Donoghue (1983)
*Reardon Smith Line* (1984) two editions
*The South American Saint Line* (1985)
*Welsh Blockade Runners in the Spanish Civil War* (1985)
*Lamport & Holt* (1986)
*Tatems of Cardiff* (1987)
*Booth Line* (1987)
*Jack Billmeir, Merchant Shipowner* (1989)
*Welsh Shipping, Forgotten Fleets* (1989)
*The Gallant Ship 'Stephen Hopkins'* with R.J. Witt (1990)
*Palm Line* with Laurence Dunn (1994)
*Not All Coppers Are ...!* (1994)
*Wynns – The First 100 Years* for John Wynn (1995) three editions
*Wynns – The Last 20 Years* for John Wynn (1996)
*L.C. Lewis, Heavy Haulage* (1996)
*Wynns Overseas* first draft for John Wynn (1998)
*The Wynns Fleet – 120 Years of Road Haulage* (2003)
*Lamport & Holt Line* (2004)
*Road Transport Gwent* (2004)
*Road Transport – The Read Story* (2005)
*Road Transport Monmouthshire* (2005)
*Road Transport Wales & Border* (2005)
*Spanish Civil War Blockade Runners* (2006)
*Road Transport South East Wales* (2006)